BEST CONTEMPORARY
MONOLOGUES FOR WOMEN 18–35

① 11/17

BEST CONTEMPORARY MONOLOGUES FOR WOMEN 18–35

EDITED BY LAWRENCE HARBISON

THEATRE & CINEMA BOOKS

An Imprint of Hal Leonard Corporation

Published in 2014 by Applause Theatre & Cinema Books
An Imprint of Hal Leonard Corporation
7777 West Bluemound Road
Milwaukee, WI 53213

Trade Book Division Editorial Offices
33 Plymouth St., Montclair, NJ 07042

Printed in the United States of America

Book design by John J. Flannery

Library of Congress Cataloging-in-Publication Data

Best contemporary monologues for women 18-35 / edited by Lawrence Harbison.
    pages cm
 ISBN 978-1-4803-6962-7 (paperback)
 1. Monologues. 2. Acting--Auditions. 3. Women--Drama. I. Harbison, Lawrence.
 PN2080.B42 2014
 812'.6--dc23
                         2014012554

www.applausebooks.com

CONTENTS

INTRODUCTION

Here you will find close to one hundred terrific monologues for women, all from recent plays. Most have a present-tense dramatic action, because I believe these are the most effective, whether in class or for auditions. In the cases where I have included a story monologue, though, it was a great story. Some are comic (laughs), some are dramatic (generally, no laughs). Some are rather short, some are rather long.

Several of the monologues are by playwrights whose work may be familiar to you—writers such as Don Nigro, Itamar Moses, Adam Bock, Adam Rapp, Jane Martin, and David Ives. Other monologues are by exciting up-and-comers such as Nicole Pandolfo, Erik Gernand, Laura Marks, David Johnston, Crystal Skillman, Kimberly Pau, Greg Kalleres, and C. Denby Swanson. All represent the best in contemporary playwriting.

Many of the plays from which these monologues have been culled have been published previously and, hence, are readily available either from the publisher/licensor or from a theatrical bookstore such as the Drama Book Shop in New York. A few of the plays may not be published for a while, in which case you may contact the author or his or her agent to request a copy of the entire text of the play that contains the monologue that suits your fancy. Information on publishers/rights holders may be found in the Play Sources and Acknowledgments section in the back of this anthology.

Break a leg at that audition! Knock 'em dead in class!

Lawrence Harbison
Brooklyn, NY

BEST CONTEMPORARY MONOLOGUES FOR WOMEN 18–35

ABOUT SPONTANEOUS COMBUSTION
Sherry Kramer

Seriocomic
MARY CATHERINE, late 20s–early 30s

MARY CATHERINE *hasn't been home in a long time because she considers herself too sophisticated to fit in with her "all American" family. She has come back for the funeral of her Aunt Emily, who died from the shock of seeing* MARY CATHERINE's *younger sister,* AMALIA, *having sex with her boyfriend on a pile of clothing. Now,* AMALIA *refuses to get out of the bathtub. She believes that her aunt spontaneously combusted and that she will too, and that she has to be immersed in water to be safe.* MARY CATHERINE *has decided that it's her mission to get* AMALIA *out of the tub, and has gone into the bathroom to confront her.*

MARY CATHERINE   Molly, when people spend days sitting in bathtubs of cold water they catch cold. Yeah, yeah, I know you're not afraid of catching cold. You're afraid of catching hot. But basically, Molly, I believe it all comes down to a fear of catching a temperature other than your own. This is why, I freely admit, your decision to silently semidrown yourself makes no sense to me. If it is even possible to separate hot and cold, ying and yang—if it is even possible, spiritually, theoretically you still can't do it in this instance, because getting a fever is the very body to the soul of catching cold. This spontaneous combustion is just a screen, Molly. It's not what really has you scared. No. What you, Amalia Parker, are frightened of, what has you up to your neck in the wet quarter-nelson of fear is nothing more, nothing less, nothing but the common cold. For most women I know, a man represents a cure for a vital, everyday illness. But they can never quite remember whether the rule really is feed a fever and starve a cold. It sounds obvi-

1

ously onomatopoeic. And the instinct once thwarted, they end up starving the wrong mouth for the greater part of their lives. They get so busy pushing men into places inside them that are not connected to even the suggestion of a digestive tract. Well, maybe you're right. Maybe discretion is the better part of valor. If you can't say something nice, don't say anything at all, and all. You know, when we were kids I thought it said, "the better part of velour." "Discretion is the better part of velour." Ever since then I've always suspected that discretion was somehow synthetic. Counterfeit. That's what I think now, Molly. [*Pause.*] Molly, it's just not all that attractive, your sitting there all wet, not saying anything. I mean, your little mermaid routine, I can go for that. But I keep wanting to ask you if the cat's got your tongue. Tuna fish, Molly. That's what this charade suggests to me. Tuna fish. And I don't get it.

ADULT
Christine Masciotti

Dramatic
TARA, 18

TARA, a college freshman, hates where she goes to school because she thinks it's full of cardboard, cookie-cutter phonies. She has come to her father, who has a gun shop in his home in Reading, PA, basically to hang out and talk about her life. For him, Reading is a rapidly deteriorating nowheresville; for her, it's just what she needs for a while.

TARA I feel like my life is going around and around in a very small circle, and never advancing at all. I just feel like everything is so lame. I'm living a person I don't wanna be. I'm 18. I don't wanna be 80 and be like, I just did what I was supposed to. I mean college isn't what people think it is. The key to opportunity or whatever. There's so much bullshit going on. Yeah, it's great if you wanna be brainwashed into all this commercialism and money-hungry country, stay in school. I just don't see what's the point. I don't see my life going anywhere with it. What could I do in ten years? Mediocre job. High rent. Loan payments on top of everything. I wanna experience my life. I don't know. I've always been afraid of change. Right now, I want my life to turn completely upside down. Like even just being back here, I feel like a different person. I feel more of who I really am. [*Pause.*] Actually, I was thinking about taking a semester off, and maybe staying here a while. I don't know how to explain it, but I mean the second I got off the bus, I felt so connected to myself. It's beautiful. You can see the sky. There're trees. It's like so natural, like I don't need to use materialistic things to make me happy. I can see why peo-

3

ple spend their whole lives here. I don't know what I wanna do for my life, and I don't know where I wanna be ten years from now, but right now, I wanna be here. I wanna be in the middle of nowhere. So, what do you think?

ADULT
Christine Masciotti

Dramatic
TARA, 18

TARA has left her freshman year at college to decide what she wants to do with her life. She has been living with her father. Turns out, she has a boyfriend whom she wants to go and visit, but she needs bus fare to get there. Her father, not happy with her choice of boyfriend, doesn't want to give it to her.

TARA   You never reached out to me. You sent birthday gifts through snail mail so they came a week late. You think that counts for anything? It's more-personal communication like using Skype or FaceTime that makes a difference. How dare you stop paying child support when I turned eighteen? You washed your hands about me. All you do is pay my phone bill! You buy me a phone for my birthday, something from the dinosaur time—you didn't even pay twenty dollars for it. I looked it up on eBay and the bidding started at ninety-nine cents! After a year of dry spell, you look for extra work. It doesn't work that way—the bills keep coming in. You have to find work. You're not the only one with financial problems! You took money under the table not to pay child support! We had to petition the court. Checks came. Eleven dollars. Twenty-four dollars. I don't know why Mom endorsed them . . . fold and tear, fold and tear, fifteen dollars! Wow! Thanks, Dad! Mom was starting a business on her own. One person worked for her who she couldn't pay. We had to move to pay for my first semester of college. We had to move to a smaller place. You didn't pay for my education. One thing I need your help with, and you can't do it! I didn't know how lucky I was to be spared any fucking connection to you.

AEROSOL DREAMS
Nicole Pandolfo

Seriocomic
MARIA, 20s

MARIA *is talking to* TOMMY, *the bartender in a joint in New Jersey, with whom she has had sex with the night before, about her former fiancée,* DANNY, *who died tragically in a fall.*

MARIA   Don't remind me about Danny. I just . . . don't understand people. Like, why do they pretend one thing with you, only to need something totally different? Anyway, I'd rather be alone, really. It's so much easier. [*A beat.*] Do you ever feel like . . . like I don't know. That you missed something that was important? Like on the way you choose left instead of right and missed the way you were supposed to go. Like somehow you accidentally fucked it all up? But you can't figure out how or where or when it went wrong? [*A beat.*]

Fucking cigarettes. I just had to go get cigarettes. [*A long pause.*] If I hadn't left, maybe we would have went inside. I would have sat on his lap and had another glass of champagne. Maybe we would have went into the bathroom to fuck. We used to like to do that. Have sex in people's bathrooms during parties. I don't know why. We weren't like that, like spontaneous, in any other circumstance, but we liked to fuck in people's bathrooms during parties. [*A pause.*] We would have gotten married last week. If it hadn't—you know, if he wasn't dead. Right when I got my ticket to Newark. I was packing my bags to come home about when I would have been packing them to go on my honeymoon. And get this. We were gonna go to Vegas. And get married again by Elvis. We both really wanted to do that—to get married by Elvis—but his mom had a fit and wanted it to be a Catholic wedding, but we both really wanted Elvis. So we were gonna do it. Do both. Catholic wedding in New York and then a honeymoon in Vegas. [*A beat.*] I just love Elvis. And what's fucked up about life . . . Fate . . . The Stars . . . Whateverthefuck is ruling this god-damn circus—is that I was in Vegas. I went to Vegas. Only there was no Elvis. And no Danny. But I was there just when I was supposed to be. Somehow. Do you think I'll ever feel better?

AMERICA'S BRIGHTEST STAR

Alex Goldberg

Comic
AMBER, early 20s

After having sex with CECIL RAVINSDALE, *the host of the TV talent competition* America's Brightest Star, AMBER *asks* CECIL *to rank her performance. He does, and it's not kind. After he finishes his harsh critique, which nearly leaves her in tears,* AMBER *strikes back.*

AMBER   You have a small penis. You do. It is below average. What was that, four inches while hard? And not very thick. If you're going to be four inches, at least give me a little something to work with, so I feel something. I may be young, but I have seen seven penises so far . . . well, eight now, and you know where you rank? Seventh. John Baker had a smaller penis, but the only time I was with him he sort of came really quickly while he was semihard, so I'm not really sure. You could be the smallest. No wonder you put your underwear back on right away. To hide the evidence. Which was already pretty well hidden. And what's with the grunting? More like a squeal. I'm not trying to be rude, but you sounded like my little brother's guinea pig when it was hungry and begging for food. What kind of man sounds like that? And you don't smell very good. I don't care if it's Jordan by Michael Jordan. It stinks. And your balls stink. Maybe I would have blown you for longer if you smelled a little better. On a scale of 1 to 10, 10 being Ryan Gosling and 1 being Jeff Horkins, who is my brother's idiot friend, I'd give you negative eight million. You definitely rank eighth out of eight. And I can't wait to tell my viewers. Good day, sir.

AMERICA'S BRIGHTEST STAR
Alex Goldberg

Comic
AMBER, early 20s

AMBER *records her latest entry in her* VLOG, *a video diary she uploads to the Internet. In previous* VLOG *entries she talks about her plan to move to Hollywood and become a famous celebrity. This is her first entry after making the arrangements to make it to Hollywood.*

AMBER   I have some very exciting news. So, Mr. Producer man . . . well, he begged to see me, and guess what?

[*She beats out a drumroll on her leg.*]

He's taking me to Hollywood! Yep, the big city and me! The next time I film this VLOG, I'll be coming to you from my glamorous new digs in sunny Southern California. This week will be my last here in this town, so don't panic if I go a few weeks without updating. I won't be staying with him, of course, but I'm sure his guest house will do nicely. I couldn't have done it without all your help. I want you all to know that you are my closest friends, and I cherish all the time I've spent talking to you, and reading your responses. Your support has been wonderful, and it's on the strength of your backs that has enabled me to stand so tall. I'd also like to thank my agent and everyone at the studio, who were all very helpful in getting my career going. Let's see, all my wonderful costars, who made me look better every day. Of course, I made them look great from day one! Oh, I had so many more people to thank, but now that I'm actually up here, I don't really remember everything! Ugh . . . my acting coach would kill me for blanking. I must thank the loves of my life, of course, my dogs Bipsy and Nipsy. Boys, mama's bringing you steak tomorrow! And lastly, I know, the music is kicking in, but just give me a few more seconds please, thanks . . . And lastly, all of you, because if none of you had watched me, if none of you had tuned into my early days of having a VLOG, then I wouldn't exist. Without you, I don't exist.

ANATOMIES
Don Nigro

Seriocomic
MARY, 19

MARY PATTERSON, *a beautiful young prostitute on the streets of Edinburgh in the late 1820s, is in love with a young doctor who works for a famous anatomist, dissecting corpses. The young doctor loves her but is reluctant to rescue her from her career on the streets, in fear of ruining his career. She is bitter and angry, and hurt, but here she tries to drown her hopes of marriage and a normal life and see her profession as empowering.*

MARY   Getting hurt is just life. I don't care. I'm a strong girl. At worst, I'll end up the best old whore in Edinburgh. I'm not going to worry about men any more, ever. Drown all the babies and rake in the money. Then when I get to Heaven, I'll have enough cash to bribe my way in. And then no more relations with Mary Patterson. A palace in Heaven and no more relations. I've seen the light now, Janet. Maybe I did let myself believe a fellow loved me, but it's all clear now. I won't be foolish any more about it. The way I see it, there's no harm in whoring. The body is just a big, smelly thing the soul is trapped in. And Lord knows, we can't profit off the beauty of our bodies very long, so we might as well make the most of it while it's still a moneymaker. Beauty doesn't last. Joy doesn't last. Liquor doesn't last. Not that I wouldn't get out of it if I could. But then I think, what's the difference? We're all whores of one sort or another. A certain young man I know would have us believe we're just a heap of guts inside and no more than that. The body's just something to be used. And everybody does. He uses it. Why shouldn't I make a living off it? If you don't own your own body, what do you own? And if you can't make a living off your own flesh, what have you got? The sons of bitches have taken everything else from us. Do they want to own our bodies and our souls both?

ANATOMIES
Don Nigro

Seriocomic
MARY, 19

MARY PATTERSON, *a beautiful young prostitute on the streets of Edinburgh in the late 1820s, in despair over her rejection by a young doctor who loves her but can't risk destroying his career by marrying her, has allowed herself to be lured to the lodgings of Burke and Hare, who are in the business of murdering the poor and selling their corpses to Dr. Knox's anatomy class for dissection. It's late at night, MARY's been given enough liquor to lower her suspicions, and now she is getting into bed, believing that all her companion, the sullen giant Hare, wants from her is copulation. In fact, when she is asleep, he will strangle her so he can sell her body to the anatomist. These are her last living moments.*

MARY   Well, then, I suppose I'd better start earning my keep, if I'm going to stay. I don't want anybody saying Mary Patterson didn't earn her keep. Lord, it's cold tonight. Under the covers we go. This is not such a terrible bed, considering some of the places I've slept. It's better than huddling under trash bins in the alley. On a cold night like this, sometimes I just want to curl up in a warm bed and never wake up. Or wake up in Heaven. Or sleep a thousand years, and wake up someplace where it's warm. It's never warm enough in Edinburgh, at least not for me, except when it's too hot. You'd better get me while you can, Mr. Hare, for I'm drifting off fast. Unless you like your women to be snoring. Don't be shy, Mr. Hare. Are you shy? You're a big, strong fellow, aren't you? I must warn you that I have bad dreams, too. I dream about the filthy streets and alleys that I wander in. Dirty places, horrible dreams. In my dreams, I'm lost, and can't be found. And then I wake up, and I haven't been dreaming at all. I wonder what the Queen of France dreams about. Do you know what I'd do, if I was the Queen of France? First, I'd kill the King. Then I'd kill all the doctors. We'd all live a good deal longer if there were no doctors. They feed on death. Like ghouls. Doctors are ghouls. Do you think we get to keep our bodies in Heaven, Mr. Hare? Because I don't think I want mine. Although other people might. I'm told it's quite a nice body, and sometimes I am fond of it, looking in shop windows at it, but I think I'd rather just be a breath of air. Just a mouthful of air on a June morning is all I'd like to be. Just a mouthful of air.

ANY DAY NOW
Nat Cassidy

Comic
JACKIE, early 20s

At the start of the play, small numbers of the recently deceased have begun reanimating and rising from their graves, and now the media and the public at large are disturbed and confused as to what this phenomenon means. Unlike the zombies of pop entertainment, however, these "returned decedents" have so far proven to be completely harmless. Just conscious-less, walking corpses; that is, until a frustrated local Connecticut politician, BEVERLY COLBY-PARKER, *claims that the reanimated corpse of her father has just attacked and bitten her. She is rushed to the hospital amid a media frenzy and quickly embraces her newfound fame by holding passionate press conferences to growing crowds on the steps of the hospital, calling for martial law to destroy these so-called monsters. In this scene at the top of Act Two, while* BEVERLY *is still in the hospital, her daughter* JACKIE *(who was just expelled from college for selling weed) visits* APRIL, BEVERLY's *sister, in the family's kitchen, where the entirety of the play takes place.*

JACKIE   Everything I know has been through the news, or whatever. I haven't gotten the chance to talk to her at all—she's never there when I call. [*Beat.*] This has all worked out pretty well for her, though, right? Rinky-dink little shit politician from nowhere, and now look at her. Like, not two weeks, and she's already, what, like a spokesperson? I'm hearing her name used as, like, a reference. I see her face on CNN, with her stupid fucking doctor, and her stupid fucking arm: "Our government must act now!" rah-rah-rah. With that smile—ugh. I call it the shark mouth. The way it just doesn't quite reach her eyes, you know? So vapid and insincere. Creeps me out. [*Beat. A realization.*] She's like the Paris Hilton of the zombie apocalypse. Think about it. Professor Matos says that Paris Hilton represents the culmination of the undoing of feminism through the embrace of victimization. Fame was literally thrust into her—it wasn't until a forcible injection of the masculine that she was deemed worthy of our attention. She's celebrated for being a receptacle for semen. A gift bestowed by the patriarchy. Ipso facto, mom has become a sensation solely because of also being penetrated by a man. Granted, by his teeth, but . . . [*A longing sigh.*] Have I told you about Professor Matos yet? He's the greatest professor of all time. It's true! I had him for that Problems of Evil class I told you about? Critical Cultural Concepts? He changed my life. "Man, so long as he lives, has no more constant and agonizing anxiety than to find someone to worship as soon as possible." It's Dostoevsky. "The Grand Inquisitor." We were reading it when I got the ol' . . . [*She cocks a thumb back and blows a raspberry: her expulsion.*] Professor Matos just sent me an e-mail with the page number and a message saying, "Bet this is starting to ring some bells." He's so funny. Isn't that perfect? I'm thinking of getting it tattooed it on my chest, right here, so that next time Mom has a little rally, I can flash my tits at the cameras and get the message out.

THE ASK
David Lee White

Comic
SALLY, mid-20s to mid-30s

SALLY *has just joined the board of her local theater and has taken* DARREN *out to dinner in order to ask him for a $10,000 contribution. She is completely unaware that* DARREN's *wife has recently died. After* SALLY *makes "the ask,"* DARREN *tells her that he thought they were on a date. Humiliated,* SALLY *tries to turn the situation around and begins seducing* DARREN *by telling him how much she loves the theater.*

SALLY   I want this. I mean maybe I want this. Actually, for sure, I am definitely, maybe ready for a relationship. I mean we've got some differences to overcome, sure. We're from different worlds and all that. I'm a simple girl that lives within my means, you know? And you're an extraspecial rich guy with golf clubs and snow-globe doorknobs and Monet paintings in the bathroom. But you gotta know something about me. Sometimes, I'm fucking crazy. Like really emotionally needy, like cry-for-no-reason crazy. But—BUT—it's only because I'm so full of passion! And here's something you gotta know about me. I mean if we're gonna be together, this is something you have to learn to embrace. I love art. Love it. Look at me in the fucking eyes and you'll be able to see how serious I am. Serious like cancer. Sorry. A heart attack. I love everything about art. And you know what the best art is? Theater. I love the way it makes me feel. I love the way it frees my mind. I love the way it breaks down the walls of convention and makes us ask questions that we never dared to ask. I love the messed-up red chairs that hurt my ass and the pretentious production photos in the lobby. I love the stupid sweatshirts and the overpriced Shakespeare paperbacks in the gift shop. But most of all, I love the people that make theater. I love how they cuss in front of each other in the workplace like it's something to be proud of. I love how the actors flirt with each other and give one another unnecessary backrubs. I love how they can go from laughing to crying in about two seconds and mean absolutely every bit of it. I love how they eat nothing but couscous but still manage to smoke enough cigarettes to choke a pack-mule. I love how they blame everyone else for the fact that they don't make enough money. I love how the directors scream and insult everyone they meet so they can sound smarter and more passionate than the rest of us. I love the theater technicians that absolutely refuse to do anything productive until they've bitched for at least an hour. I love that. My God, I more than just love those people. I want to be those people. I want to live my life on the edge. I want to have sex that I only barely remember. I want to argue about politics and pretend that I watch the news. I want to complain that there's no cot in the dressing room. I want to be difficult and cranky and have bags under my eyes and a constant, small, hacking cough that spreads through the entire cast until it becomes pneumonia. So are you ready Darren? Are you ready to take that leap with me? Are you ready to be on that fucked-up roller-coaster for the rest of your life?

BARRIO HOLLYWOOD
Elaine Romero

Dramatic
GRACIELA: 29, Latina

GRACIELA MORENO *is a ballet folklórico dancer. Her younger brother ALEX received a head injury while boxing, and his doctors do not expect him to survive. By this point in the play ALEX has died, and the police suspect that his mother has mercy-killed him. Here, they are interrogating GRACIELA about what she may know about this suspected murder.*

GRACIELA   We all wanted to believe. See, where I come from, if you have faith, God has pity on you and makes things better. It's like He reaches His hand into your head and captures whatever picture you hold there. And if you imagine it just right, He'll set His hand down on Earth and set that picture free. He makes it real. But you've got to believe. That's the first rule of faith. I told my mother we could imagine Alex healthy. Just like she taught me. We would create this powerful image of him. I could see him right there. So beautiful. [*Beat. Frustrated.*] I don't know where it went. Has that ever happened to you? Someone you love dies and you just can't see them anymore? [*Beat.*] My mother? She does what she wants.

[*Realizing she's incriminated Amá.*]

Well, she wants the best for us. Me and Alex. That's all I meant.

[*She offers her hands.*]

Here. Why don't you arrest me instead? I love my amá. I'd do anything for her, so go ahead. You found her. At St. Augustine's Cathedral downtown. Well, it was Sunday morning. Before four a.m.? Please. Have pity on her. My mother's practically a *viejita*. [*Short beat.*] Well, we get old fast *en mi barrio*. [*Beat.*] Her going to confession doesn't mean a thing. She goes every week. She always thinks she's got some great sin. She went to confession for breaking the garbage disposal. She went to confession for cheating at poker. She went to confession for taking God's name in vain the day Alex fell in the ring. But who should be confessing here? Maybe God, himself, should go to confession for taking His sword and piercing it straight through my mother's heart?

THE BEAUTIFUL DARK
Erik Gernand

Dramatic
SYDNEY, 18

NANCY *has read a play by a schoolmate in which a kid commits a school shooting. She reported this to her principal, and the kid has been expelled. Now she tells the principal that she feels guilty.*

SYDNEY   It was his play. He was writing it on his own, like in-stead of doing homework and stuff. And for like the whole semester it was all he worked on. But he wouldn't let me read it, or even talk about it. He was obsessed with this play and I wanted to know why. To see in his head. Sometimes he just gets so quiet, you know? So we were in his room one time and he went to take a shower. And I knew I had like fifteen minutes at least, so I got on his computer . . . and I know I shouldn't, it wasn't my business . . . but I emailed it to myself. So that night I read his play. And it scared me. You know Jacob. I mean he gets angry . . . you know, moody, pissy sometimes. But this play . . . his play. It was just different. Violent. Really violent. About school. And it just seemed so personal. I mean, I think everything people write is personal, but this seemed like it was more than that. Next week is Jacob's birthday. And the kid in his story . . . that's when the guy does it I had this feeling . . . you know? You hear stories. On the news. When bad things happen. And everybody says they didn't know. I mean, maybe they thought the guy was acting kind of strange, but they didn't really know. Not what the guy would do at least. Like with that congresswoman in Arizona. Or Virginia Tech. What if they knew but they just didn't want to know? I'm probably totally wrong. I didn't know what to do, though. So I told my adviser. I gave her the play. I didn't know they were going to kick him out. I swear. I wanted them to help him. Why didn't they help him?

BETHANY
Laura Marks

Seriocomic
CRYSTAL, late 20s

CRYSTAL *is a saleswoman at a Saturn dealership. She is speaking to a recalcitrant, slightly odd customer who may or may not want to buy a car.* CRYSTAL *really needs to close the deal, as she is practically destitute.*

CRYSTAL   What our customers have found is that the places that say they negotiate are really just jacking up the price to begin with, so that's the great thing about Saturn: total price transparency. We put it all right there on a sheet of paper. I might be able to throw in some free Saturn merchandise. But if buying American is something that doesn't matter to you, then I don't know what else I can say. If you want to buy something that came from a factory in Oki-saka-whatever, then go right ahead. But when you buy a Saturn, you're buying American ingenuity and American jobs; from the person who hands you the keys all the way back to the guys on the line in Spring Hill, Tennessee—it's like a family. And when you buy a Saturn, you can feel yourself becoming a part of that family. Charlie, I don't think you're really undecided. I think you know exactly what you want to do. I've told you about the features of this car until I'm blue in the face. So you want to know how this car is going to change your life. Oh, Charlie. You've hit on the exact reason why I love selling cars. Because other than a house, I think a car is the single most life-enhancing purchase a person can make. Your car is like a second skin. You're in it every day. You live in it, you escape in it, you can even sleep in it . . . I've done that. If you have a family, it can change your relationship with your kids. If you're a single guy, it can be the thing that gets you laid. It's the face you show the world. It's you.

BIKE AMERICA
Mike Lew

Dramatic
PENNY, 27

This monologue comprises the final scene of Bike America. PENNY, our plucky protagonist, has just spent the last three months on a cross-country bike trip from Boston to Santa Barbara. She'd never lived anywhere but at school or her parents' place, and she'd been hoping the trip would help her to find herself, and to find a place that feels more like home. Instead, she finds her life and her trip cut short when she is run over by a truck while biking alone in the night in the middle of the Arizona desert. In a direct address to the audience, PENNY now wrestles with what, if anything, she's learned from the journey.

PENNY What's up you fuckers I'm dead. Do I have any regrets? Yes. Would I do it again? No.

The truck driver phoned in the accident just after he *awoke from the wheel*. That was thoughtful. He realized he'd turned his fifty-three-foot trailer into a forty-four-thousand pound penny-crushing machine. You remember those penny-crushing machines they have at museums where you put in fifty-one cents and out comes a flattened penny shaped like a scenic vista? That's pretty much the deal with me. After the usual freak-outs, the group pressed on and found the Pacific. They dipped their raw, weary feet in the waves and mumbled platitudes like, "Penny really would've liked this." And I'm like—yes. Yes, I would've liked this. I would've liked this a great deal more than being *smeared out like toothpaste* on the Arizona highway. And I felt these waves of regret at being a fuckup. And I felt these waves of regret at all the time I spent looking outwards, all that deflection when I should have just loved and lived. And I could have loved. Anyone. And I could have lived. Anywhere. Anywhere down that four-thousand mile expanse. There were four thousand Pennies all down that route, and yet I had to go and pick that one. They stood there, their feet in the sand, feeling the waves that I'd never feel, watching a sunset I'd never see. And they smiled and nodded like they knew me. And I thought, how could they know me? I still don't know me.

BITE ME
Nina Mansfield

Comic
ELLEN, mid-20s to mid-30s

ELLEN *has managed to subdue a vampire with pepper spray (who knew you could do that?) and has brought him home in a cage. Her husband has told her he wants them to spend all eternity together. Here's his chance.*

ELLEN   So there he is, stunned from the spray. Writhing on the ground like a baby. When WHAM! Got him in the balls. BAM, I hit him with my handbag, and ZANG, got him again with the pepper spray. At that point it was like pure adrenaline! I was on fire! Once I had him subdued I realized the emblem on my Tory Burch handbag is totally cross-like, so I held it up to his face, and sure enough he was like, *Ahh*, and I was like, "Take that, you creature of the dark," and he was like, *Ahhh*, and I was like, "That's what you get for attacking women in alleys," and he's like, *Please, I can't help it! It's just my nature*, and I'm like, "I don't care if it's just your nature, you woman hater," and he's like, *Please, I don't hate women, I just want to suck your blood*, and I'm like "Eew," and he's like, *You get used to it*, and I'm like "Really?" and he's like, *Really*, and then he started to lunge for me again, 'cause I'd sort of forgotten to hold up my handbag, but I was like really caffeinated, so my reflexes were on point, so I was like, "Take this!" and he was like, *Ahhh*. And then I had this idea. I thought, why not take lemons and turn them into lemonade? I was like, "You scumbag vampire," and he was like, *I'm really not a scumbag*, and I was like, "Oh yeah?" and he was like, *Yeah*, and so I sprayed him with more pepper spray, and made him drape my handbag over his shoulder, which made him lose like all his powers, and then I loaded him into the back of the Escalade and voila!

BLACKTOP SKY
Christina Anderson

Dramatic
IDA: 18, African American

IDA is talking to her boyfriend WYNN *about the four-building housing project where she lives.*

IDA   Fucking neighborhood stinks in the summer. All this heat. Don't matter anyway. Everybody sees everything, but they don't care. Everybody is always out, in the streets. Day and night. People on stoops, leaning on cars, hanging out of windows. You can't get away from nobody. Building 1 . . .

[*Ida turns in the direction of the first building.*]

. . . See? There's Mr. Wheeler smoking up, reading the paper. Building 3 . . .

[*Turns in the direction of the third building.*]

. . . Sasha is on the phone running her mouth. Building 4 . . .

[*Turns.*]

. . . Mrs. James is greasing her scalp. Building 2 . . .

[*Turns.*]

. . . My mama is sitting up there sleeping. Four buildings make up this project. And every building got seven floors. And every floor got eleven windows going across it. All those windows facing down to this courtyard, those benches. So Mr. Wheeler was smoking. So Sasha was talking bullshit. Mrs. James was sitting by the window, listening to the radio. But nobody said nothing to me. Nobody asked me anything. Am I crazy? I don't know if I'm crazy. Don't know if I'm making shit up. Am I cracking out? Sitting up in my dingy-ass apartment, hiding out from what? From who? Something I made up? Must've. Had to have made it up 'cause nobody said nothing. It wasn't nothing. Nothing for me to sprint pass these benches every day. This is the only way out to the street, Wynn. When I leave my building, I have to cross through here to get to the street. Every other exit is blocked by a fence with a thick chain and fat padlock keeping it shut. I can't even choose how I come and go. I'm glad I met you downtown at a movie theater. Nowhere near here cause otherwise I'd only see all this [*Re the projects.*] when I look at you. But I don't. I don't, Wynn. And that's why I like you. That's why I need you. [*Pause.*] I'm going home. I'll talk to you later.

BLACKTOP SKY
Christina Anderson

Dramatic
IDA: 18, African American

*IDA is talking to KLASS, a young man who lives on a bench in the
projects where she lives, about a demonstration she has just been to.*

IDA   !! Justice for our Streets !!
   !! Justice means Peace !!

Klass, oh my god, Klass, you shoulda seen it! People everywhere! Signs everywhere! Speeches! Chants! Shit, I should
protest more often. I feel good!! You should start one. You
should make a sign, then go down and call out those ignorant muthafucks sittin' in those big offices. Shame those
ignorant money whores who are only interested in helping
A people not THE people, you know? They only interested
in a certain kind of people who don't LOOK nothin' like me
or you. Who don't LIVE like me or you. ESPECIALLY you. Go
down there and bust some knowledge in the face of those
dudes who makin' your life so hard. Got you out here livin'
like this. We need to get you down there, Klass. But, but
you need a chant though. We need to write a good one for
you. You gotta yell something in repetition. Make it have a
rhythm to it. Not too many words. Gotta be simple and to
the point. So those cash hoes know what you saying. They
gotta know what you're willing to do for your rights. For
your justice. It's gotta be short 'cause the more you say your
chant, the more you believe it. You start yelling it. Getting
loud!! And you feel it coming from your toes, your nose,
your, your lips, your eyeballs:

!! Justice for our Streets !!
!! Justice means Peace !!

This is how it's going down: I'll make signs. One for me. One for you. And T-shirts. We can make those together. We'll make T-shirts. These [*Re: the one she's wearing.*] cost ten bucks or some shit. We'll make some T-shirts. We'll go in the streets and keep marching and chanting 'til they right the wrongs!

BOB: A LIFE IN FIVE ACTS
Peter Sinn Nachtrieb

Comic
JEANINE, 20s

JEANINE *has just discovered a baby* (BOB) *in the bathroom of the restaurant where she works and has fallen in love with him and taken him. While driving, she tries to explain her reasons why.*

JEANINE   I was finishing up my Sunday night dinner at the Bamboo Wok. I don't know how authentic or healthy it is, but I like the flavors. I'd been working my way through the menu for about a year. Each week, I would have a new entrée in order of appearance. I'd finally made it to the Noodles-slash-Rice section after several months of Lamb and I felt like I was entering a new era in my life. When the waiter delivered the check and cookie, the fortune inside seemed different. The paper looked shiny, almost golden, the ink darker, more insistent. "You will be the mother to a great great man." The fortunes I usually get are a little more vague than that. But this felt intentional. Like someone was watching me. From inside the cookie. It made me smile. I thought "Well, cool, Jeanine—maybe the future isn't only selling tiny burgers and having Asian food once a week." And then my stomach started to twitch, felt like I was gonna be sick. I started sweating, breathing heavy. And I thought, "Oh my god, it's happening already." I stood up from my table and shouted, "I'm gonna be the mother to a great great man!" Next thing I knew I woke up in a hospital bed. At first I thought I'd conceived my great man immaculate till the nurse told me that I'd almost died at the restaurant. That I had a severe reaction to the gluten in Asian noodles-slash-rice that messed up my insides so much that I would never be able to make a "Great Great Man" the regular way. I don't really care for fortunes very much anymore. But, funny, you know, there you are. There you are. I will give you food and shelter. I will educate you. I will make sure that becoming President of the United States remains a possibility. Even if it kills me, I will make you a great great man.

BRIDGE AND TUNNEL
Anne Flanagan

Comic
NIKKI, 20s–30s

NIKKI *is in a bar with her friend* TIFFANY. TIFFANY *has asked* NIKKI *how many times she has gone out with a guy* NIKKI *has recently started dating.* NIKKI *has found a woman's shoe in the guy's apartment.*

NIKKI   First I find some random woman's shoe under his bed and then Tom acted really weird when I brought up the future of our relationship and we've already been out three times!! Plus four phone conversations—one that was like fifty-five minutes—so really, we've been out 4.6 times and we've had sex twice—both on date three, which, as I said, was really date 4.6 so it's not like I'm a slut and we had a real connection but now I don't know what to think! I thought he lived alone; although he is a teacher and he probably doesn't make that much money so maybe he has a roommate—but he never mentioned one and I know he's got a daughter but she lives with her mom and I don't think this was his weekend unless maybe they switched weekends, but I think she's like ten and this is not the shoe of a ten-year-old. Maybe his daughter was there and his ex came to pick her up and she lost the shoe—but what, then she just left with one shoe? Like, you'd notice something like that, right? It's not an earring. Those, sure, they get lost without you noticing, but a shoe? No one loses a shoe and doesn't know it unless they're totally stoned. Oh My God, what if his ex was there and she was totally stoned—what if they were both high? It's like a aphrodisiac after all and what if they— OH MY GOD! Is this his ex's shoe? Would he tell me? Was she there? Are they TOGETHER? Or is it something else entirely?!

BROADWAY OR BUST
Rosary O'Neill

Dramatic
SUSAN, 17–26

SUSAN, *a breast cancer survivor, is trying out for a part on Broadway. Here, she talks to the auditioner.*

SUSAN   I want to live to seventy or eighty or fifty. I don't
see why I have to talk about my illness to get cast in your
show . . . I don't want to go back there, because it's a long
road it's not just remove THIS—it's a panoply of choices
and any one could kill you. No one tells you how com-
plicated it is, 'cause you'd be scared out of your mind. I
just want to act. Get to Broadway. I don't have time for
mindless chatter. Take me to dinner and I'll jabber away.
I need backup because with *Team Love* we can really pop
open this room. I'm one of six children, the *unpreferred*
one. Just 'cause I'm pretty and a girl doesn't mean I can't
be direct. I don't want people dumping my pictures and
resumes into garbage after I . . . because acting is my
opiate against death. If I go to Broadway, I won't die.
Look at me. It's the theater community I'm after. There
are people dying. There are people being born. But I have
died before I died. So Broadway has to let me in. This is
the last irrelevant thing I'm going to say. I'm an actor with
a life-threatening disease and still I got to . . . face these
extended, labyrinthian auditions. Maybe this callback will
cause a relapse. Or steal my beauty years. Do you know
what's it like to fear a slow death? I'm an artist, someone
trained to think in images, to become deeply sensitive.
I'm scared to lift my arm and find some strange pain or
new lump or weird bruise. I can't go back to life where

it's struggle, struggle, struggle. Sorry we don't need you, you're not right, maybe next time. I got to trick my mind, replace the bad thoughts, make myself dream a future. Give me the part.

BROKEN FENCES

Steven Simoncic

Dramatic
APRIL, mid-30s

APRIL has convinced her husband CZAR to move into a gentrifying neighborhood in the heart of Chicago's deep West Side. The neighborhood has proven to be dangerous. This monologue is her self-audit of how she got here and why she made this choice. It is delivered to the audience.

APRIL   am invisible. Been invisible all my life. When I was a kid, I could go days, weeks, without being seen. Dirty-brown dishwater hair and flat-ironed features wrapped in bad posture and functional shoes. A "B student" with a "B cup" from a sanitized suburb whose most extraordinary feat was a perfect-attendance plaque and a Charlie Hustle Award at basketball camp. An upper-middle-class, middle-of-the-bell-curve, too-quiet-to-be-tragic, too-boring-to-be-bulimic, forgettable flavor with an academic-alcoholic dad and a trophy-wife mom. So I tried to make myself be seen. From slut, to goth, to punk, to priss, to princess, to yogi. I hijacked identities and wore personalities like Catholic schoolgirl skirts. Until they had to see me—incomplete and stereotypical, silly and pathetic—like a dreamcatcher on a dashboard or a tattoo of the word "hubris" on the small of your back. Search and destroy, damn the torpedoes, cut your forearm with a kitchen knife and blow away a coffee-stained guidance counselor . . . be seen, be obscene, be witnessed, be intervened . . . until one day an ordinary man makes an extraordinary effort to make you feel smart and pretty. Enjoy being seen through his eyes. Stop sleeping with his friends and start sleeping with him. Get bored, get routine, get for granted, get honest about the fact that you never stopped being invisible . . . until a little stick turns blue and forty-six chromosomes turn you inside out for the whole world to see . . . Transform. Transcend. With your thick hair and your swollen ankles—your bloody gums and your linea nigra—until who you are is no longer what you were. A tangible, fragile, dirty-brown dishwater B-student, B-cup . . . mommy . . . something singular and specific, authentic and committed . . . drunk with responsibility and dripping with identity. Find a house that looks nothing like the one you grew up in. Force the issue. Fake the answer. Convince *an ordinary man who makes an extraordinary effort* that you are right . . . even if you aren't sure. Because . . . for once . . . you *need* a place to be seen.

BROKEN FENCES
Steven Simoncic

Dramatic
D: late 20s, African American

D COLEMAN *and her fiancée,* HOODY, *have lived in Garfield Park their whole lives. As the neighborhood gentrifies, their property taxes have increased and they can no longer afford to live in their own home. This is* D*'s recounting of her life and struggle for survival that continues to this very day. It is delivered to the audience.*

D I am invisible. Been invisible all my life . . . spent years moving through the shadows and cracks of broken men and angry boys too proud to ask for help . . . and too arrogant to say thank you when you give it to them anyway. Fierce, black and strong, I watched the pride lion puff up and go out into the wasteland only to come home and explode. 64. Fantastic, tragic fireworks filled with bravado and machismo, his wives and daughters, circling his fire, soothing his burns, stroking his face, and whispering sweet relief between the pounding in his ears. And when the noise stops, and the darkness fills the room, I show up, like I always do . . . in the shadows and the silence, with a bucket and a mop. Bandage a baby brother's bloody hand . . . Steady daddy as he pisses Hennessey into a jelly jar 'cause he's too drunk to stand. I clean up the glass. Lock the door. And turn off the light. Then I wrap my feet in Vaseline and impossibly puffy white socks, and I disappear under my sheets. My ashy skin now soft and serene. Because I do not need to be seen. [*Beat.*] I need to be heard. From baby cry to lullaby life isn't what you see. It is what you hear. And when you a two-month cocoa-brown baby girl left alone in a second-story walk-up, you need to be heard. So I cried until they heard me. And when your cousin takes you under the freeway, and no one can hear you over the roar of the trucks on The Kennedy, you need to be heard. So I screamed until they found me . . . until I found my own voice. Simple and clear. Louder than you'd expect. And it was *fierce* . . . almost beautiful. But now . . . I have gone silent once again. Six community meetings and three trips to the Cook County Assessor and I still cannot be heard. Two loan officers and a local news reporter . . . *and I still cannot be heard*. A half hour alone with a tax bill and an alderman . . . and I still cannot be heard. So every night I come home tired and hoarse—having lost my voice again—to say good night to a proud man who always listens but doesn't always hear. And when the house goes quiet, and the night is silent, I whisper . . . to momma. Tiny prayers and promises of survival that sound only like me. Because I know she can hear me . . . and I know she loves the sound of my voice.

A COMMON MARTYR
Michael Weems

Dramatic
MADDIE, 20–25

MADDIE returns from a shopping trip and springs her new lingerie and confessions upon RANDALL, who has secretly hooked up with MADDIE but continues flirting with her sister, LEE.

MADDIE   This is my seventy-five dollar bra. You like it? Correction. This is my seventy-five dollar "love me, fuck me, or at least goddamn notice me" bra. Did it get your attention? Because it seems like nothing else will. I thought you were different and you thought I was one of the guys. But you knew better. I was gracious to a fault. Forgiving. "Maddie doesn't mind if we talk about butts and racks and who goes down faster than a knock-kneed goalie." What would Lee have been for you, Randall? A conquest? Would she be the one who drove sixty miles in a thunderstorm to see your game? Or the one, who no matter how many times you struck out or sat on the bench, still thought you were a good player? Would she be the girl who spent hours with you at the batting cage on a Friday night, pumping tokens into that damn machine and *still* saying, "Good job." Are you going to miss me when you're gone? Probably not. In a few years and trying to start a career and you're bored with some trophy wife—I won. I think that's the moment when you realize that you actually love me. Who am I kidding? It's water off a duck's back. I'm a consolation prize. Do you deny it? Did I make you crawl into my tent? And did you think I would be your little secret—someone you can only treat like a girl when the lights are out and nobody's watching? You honestly thought the next day you could go back to "good old Maddie" and mess my hair like some little kid? I bought this getup today, thinking there might be something else for you and I. Never in my life have I spent so much on a goddamn bra. You know how I justified it? You deserved it. I may not be much to look at, but this silly thing sure makes me look filled out. Doesn't it? I used some of my graduation money. Now math isn't my strong suit. But, now that I know we won't hook up again, the ratio in my mind becomes clearer. Seventy-five dollar bra versus five inches of . . . [*She giggles.*] . . . temporary bliss.

COMPLETENESS
Itamar Moses

Dramatic
MOLLY, 20s

MOLLY, *a grad student in molecular biology, is conflicted about her feelings for* ELLIOT, *a grad student in computer science and her supposed boyfriend.*

MOLLY   This is what it's like. It's like you walk off down the road. And you think you're making all this progress. And then you stop, and look down, and you're like, oh—he is the road. And so then the question becomes: what am I supposed to do? Like, does that mean I shouldn't try again, or that I definitely should, like right away? Like, is waiting the answer, or is it the problem because the answer is not waiting? And if I don't know, then how am I supposed to tell somebody else I want to be with him and mean it? And, if I do like someone, and if that makes me forget my sadness for a while, then does that mean that that guy makes me happy? Or does that mean that, once that fades, once he's not useful anymore, for like masking or replacing all my pain, then nothing will be left, except this guy who through no fault of his own will be, like, repellent to me now, because he's just this other thing, with all of its own crap to deal with, just this extra burden on what I was carrying already? Or, if this is actually just unfixable now, if these feelings are just a part of me? Then is the right person someone who can just accept and live with them? And even if I find someone who can, what if I can't? Like, what if that's not how I want to live? Like. What if there's a place in you that's only really touched when you get hurt? And nothing else can touch you in that place. But certain things pretend they can, and so your choices are to believe until you can't anymore, and really hurt someone, and I've really hurt some people, or to keep believing, to make yourself believe, and then get hurt yourself, again, in the same place? Or does the fact that that's what all this has taught me mean that I've been doing absolutely all of it in some way wrong, that there's some other, better, way to do it, and that, every time, there is at least the chance I'll finally figure out what other way that is? [*Beat.*] You know?

CONEY
David Johnston

Dramatic
SHELLEY: 30s, lesbian

SHELLEY *sits on a bench in present-day Coney Island speaking to* MARNI, *a teenaged girl who is not getting along with her father. The two have just met.*

SHELLEY   That's the thing about The Warriors. They're trying to get back to the sea. They live in Coney. The ocean is
where they draw their strength. When they go up to the
Bronx, they're cut off. The sea is their strength. That's why
they have to get back to it. While they're by the sea, nothing can hurt them. It's their turf. All those other gangs. The
guy with the bottles on his fingers. None of that can hurt
them anymore. They've found their strength. That's what
happened to me. What happened to me is like when The
Warriors went to the gang conference in the Bronx. I left
the sea. I cut myself off from my strength. I lost who I am.
I moved to Park Slope. And I love her. I love my girl. She
wants to live in the Slope. She doesn't like Coney. She says
it's gross. I tell her it's getting better, you'll like it. But no.
She wants to be near dykes. Dyke bars. Dyke coffee shops.
Dyke herbs. Places that sell soy milk. Rice milk. Every kind
of milk except—milk. And I love her. I love the smell of her
and her taste and how she looks in the morning and I just
fucking love her. And that's something about me, when I'm
in love. I'm there. I'm a hundred and ten percent. But I made
an error. I cut myself off. From my strength. My strength did
not come from loving on that pussy. I thought it did. But it
didn't. My strength. Came from the sea. And those fucking
dykes in Park Slope. They see it. They look at me. And they

know. I don't belong. I'm not them. I've lost myself. But I can't get mad. I used to get mad, because I'd think—you know fuck you if you don't like me fuck you if I don't—like your fucking soy milk. Your fucking tea. But now I've realized. I can't be mad at them. They recognized I lost my strength. I cut myself off from the sea. I knew it when I saw *The Warriors* again last night. So I left.

CORE VALUES
Steven Levenson

Dramatic
ELIOT, early 20s

ELIOT *has had a tough time finding a job out of college, but she's just been hired by a corporate travel agency which, it turns out, is on the ropes. She is on a team-building retreat with her boss and two other employees, one of whom has just asked her about her employment history.*

ELIOT   I've been applying to probably two jobs a day for the last four months probably.

[*As* ELIOT *speaks, she begins at some point to cry.*]

But they wanted experience, all the jobs, and I don't have any experience, I guess. I mean, I went to college, and I always thought that was experience, but it's not apparently. Everywhere I go, they're like, well can you do Excel? Can you do PowerPoint? And it just gets to the point where you're like, I can't even get a job at Bed Bath & Beyond. Like literally, I tried to get a job at the Bed Bath & Beyond near Union Square and I had an interview and I thought it went pretty well, but then they never even called me back, because I didn't have enough experience. Even though I had a lot of experience in selling, in making sales, I worked at the art gallery for over three and a half months, until it *closed*, which was not my fault that the owner was a cocaine addict, but they said selling art was different, it was a different kind of skill set from home goods and they were worried I would have a hard time adjusting, in terms of skill sets. And I was, like, that's not true. And they were, like, well, we think it is true. And I was like, there are skills I have that could be

48

really valuable to you. And they were like, like what skills? And I was like, like my personality. I have a really good personality and I'm personable and I can talk to people from all walks of life and I went to a really good college and I'm smart and if you teach me how to sell home goods, I can sell home goods, I swear to God. And they were, like, we disagree. And I was like well you're totally wrong. And they were like well actually *you're* totally wrong and we're the ones who get to decide, so yeah, don't call us, we'll call you.

THE CURIOUS CASE OF THE WATSON INTELLIGENCE

Madeleine George

Seriocomic
ELIZA, 30s

ELIZA is a computer genius, intent on developing a system that will top IBM's Watson, which recently beat the three greatest Jeopardy *champions. She is talking to a computer techie who works for the Dweeb Squad, whose name happens to be* WATSON.

ELIZA   I'm actually just starting out on my own right now, so this is all still in the dream phase for the most part, but I'm developing a device that will support deep Q&A and also be highly sociable, so like, it'll answer any questions you have but it'll also ask you questions of its own, you know, in response to your emotional cues. The core of the technology is based on IBM's Watson, I don't know if you heard about the supercomputer that beat the humans on *Jeopardy* a few weeks ago? I was with Watson in the beginning. But then I left. And my system is going to be really different—it won't just be a superenhanced trivia machine. I'm working on a prototype for a low-cost, high-performance companion unit that will act as a personal advocate for people at the fringes of society. Like low-income people, nursing home patients, disabled vets. These people have been betrayed and abandoned over and over again by the very public institutions that are supposed to serve them. They need reliable, highly skilled, personalized support, a device that can get to know them better and better as it helps them navigate the social-services system. So like, you're poor, you need to go on public assistance. Instead of dragging yourself down to HRA and standing in a dehumanizing line for five hours and getting turned down anyway because you didn't fill out the stupid form right, you activate your companion device before you even leave the house. He retrieves all your documents, analyzes and leverages complex background information for you, and then, because he's fully socially enabled, entertains you if you *do* have to stand in line, and reassures you when he senses that you're distressed. The potential applications are—I mean, unfortunately—endless. People are just plummeting through the holes in the safety net, you know, all over the country—they're literally *dying* for care, and there just isn't the manpower to meet their needs. But with my device, that can all change. And of course, social justice is not exactly sexy to multinational corporations. That's why I had to strike out on my own. I want *actual* better living through technology, you know?

THE CURIOUS CASE OF
THE WATSON INTELLIGENCE
Madeleine George

Seriocomic
ELIZA, 30s

*ELIZA is a computer genius who has plans to develop a system far
superior to IBM's Watson, which beat the three* Jeopardy *champions. Here, she is having a conversation with Watson (the computer),
about her recently torrid love affair with a computer technician
from the Dweeb Squad—whose name is* WATSON.

ELIZA   Anyway it's *not* just the sex. It's that . . . this guy *knows*
me. And his learning curve is insane, I mean, I've only been
with him a few times and he already knows things about
me I didn't even know about myself. Like, the third time he
came over he brought me an LED color-changing shower-
head—I don't know if you're familiar with the technology?
You screw it in and it turns your shower into a wet and wild
disco, or that's how he described it when he was standing
there in my bathtub installing it without even asking my
permission. It's actually a pretty ingenious little piece of
engineering, and it turns out you can have a pretty great
time in there if you turn off the lights and—anyway the
point is, this is not an item I would ever, ever have brought
into my home, and how did he *know?* That I would actually
love a wet and wild disco shower? It's some kind of crazy
predictive algorithm he's running—not just mirroring; it's
enhanced, somehow. It's way more sophisticated than
anything you can do, buddy, no offense. He always knows
what I want. Half the time he gives it to me before I even
ask. And he genuinely doesn't seem to want anything in return. With Frank, everything he ever did for me was just the

opening move of some calculating transaction. This guy is . . . I would have to describe him as *preternaturally* chill. Purely, perfectly self-contained. I mean, I don't understand the mechanism. I can't begin to guess how he actually came about. And I know it sounds too I-Robot-y to be real, but I honestly can't think of any other rational explanation for what's going on. There's no way I could feel this way about a normal human guy. And you know what they say: when you have eliminated the impossible, whatever remains, however improbable, must be the truth.

CUT
Crystal Skillman

Dramatic
RENE, 31

RENE, *along with two other TV reality show writers, has been forced to cut the season finale of* The Ladies of Malibu. *Here,* RENE *is forced to face the truth of her own life falling apart as she does a "pickup interview" with* JESSICA, *one of the ladies on the show.*

RENE I'm like, "Okay, we're going to cut this interview right after you get the divorce call from your husband, so you shouldn't be smiling, okay?" And I swear to God. That grin, it doesn't come off and she's like, "What?" And I'm like, "THIS IS LIKE EMOTIONAL SHIT, OKAY? It's time to let it hang out." And she's like, "I'm getting a lot of money. The settlement." For a second I see my daughter: I see her bank account. Zero. "Maybe Jessica, you can talk more?" Maybe—maybe you can share what it's like when the man you love tells you that you are nothing like who he fell in love with? How all the affairs were your fault because you're hard and uncaring, even though you paid his fucking airfare to London with your shit job. About how in the middle of the night you cross the earth and right here—last chance—but all the time you feel Danno . . . holding you. Jessica she just: "You have to be your best self, pick yourself up, be nice to yourself in times of tragedy." There are no tears, no—and I have myself—I hate myself when my first thought is we'll have to cut in Collette's earlier footage of Jessica crying after losing her dog in her backyard for a half hour. Because the audience will need that. They want that.

[*Breaking.*]

I respect myself for knowing I can do that.

DEACTIVATED

Kimberly Pau

Seriocomic
SCHEKNA, 28

SCHEKNA *is addressing a group of couples that are competing
to be chosen to procreate. It is 2050 and the US government has
taken to controlling who is legally allowed to create life.*

SCHEKNA   Please avoid using provocative language. It's rude
and no one wants to hear it. Ask Ann—oh, Ann's not here
yet. Sorry, I didn't have breakfast. I'm. I'm sorry. I'm hungry.
Um, you are being monitored at all times. And no one is
excused from the orientation—it's mandatory. Unfortunately, I have absolutely no say about the way things go.
I'm, um, I'm, like you. Or, I don't know. Talk to me when I'm
in a better mood. Um, as I'm sure you've all experienced,
the nation has been in a state of unrest over the loss of
resources for some time. Living in underground caves is
not what paradise looked like to our ancestors and the
uncontrolled destitution in Michigan has the area classified
as condemned, but really do we know what's going on? Is
there any way to tell if the media footage hasn't been tam-
pered with? I mean, not to be cynical, um, it's true that with
the help of this program the current rate of overpopulation
based on natural resource allocation is rapidly decreasing
and the aim is to bring it down to 75 million. You might ask,
where are all the other people going to go? You tell me. I
mean, who are we calling "people" these days anyway? And
I just said that with a congressperson in the room! Which
reminds me that we are doing good work here. That's what
I have to keep telling myself, and you.

DIFFERENT ANIMALS
Abby Rosebrock

Seriocomic
MOLLY, late 20s

As MOLLY *and* JESSICA *await* JESSICA's *appointment time at the abortion clinic,* MOLLY *confesses the extent of her devotion to* JESSICA's *husband.*

MOLLY   Well, let's see. After I got fired from teaching, when I got the job at the library, I thought it'd just be awful. But then they're taking me around the office floor introducing me to people, and I see your husband sitting next to an empty cubicle. He was punching things into an old-fashioned calculator. And honestly, my first thought is: If the seat next to this man is for me, I know I'll end up falling in love with him, and I'll have to go through tons of just that crushing, unimaginable pain, but a lot of wonderful things and pure ecstasy will come out of it too, if I'm patient. And lo and behold, the seat's for me, and within weeks he's confessing things all the time; he's telling me how much he hates being broke and having dropped out of college, he feels like a failure, he misses driving out to the beach and surfing, he thinks he's too grumpy towards you. And in my head I'm thinking, Marry me, Leo! Leave your wife and let me drive you all the way out to the beach and watch you surf and let you be grumpy and show you how sexy and perfect your brain is. And one afternoon I was crying at work because I was thinking about my mom—that only happens like once a year—but Leo touched my arm to make me feel better, and he slid his hand up just a microscopic fraction of an inch underneath my sleeve. It was this short-sleeved red cardigan from Ann Taylor. I could tell he was enjoying it because we locked eyes and a tremor went through him. It was a sexual tremor; it made his fingers press into my skin. And when he felt my whole body react he laughed this quiet little laugh for a second or two because he was so proud; he knew I'd never been so turned on by anything in my life, and if it weren't for his wife he could pleasure me so much more, for however long I needed. Ever since then I've kept myself awake at night with this vision of Leo's mouth opening up to laugh. Just thinking of it—I need him to pin me down with his body and hover over me and protect me and fuck me! God . . . damn, it was his kindness that brought all this on, Jessica! His kindness to *me*! I've been with some other men, okay? I have, but Leo makes me feel the opposite of how they made me feel. I just wanna thank him, I want him so badly, Jessica, I wanna give myself to your husband so badly. I love you for being his wife, if you had children I'd love them for being his children, I love every single object you've bought together and used together! I think of all the precious little things inside your home that you depend on together, and yes I'm jealous of them, but I love them!

DIFFERENT ANIMALS
Abby Rosebrock

Seriocomic
JESSICA, late 20s

Pregnant, friendless, and freshly rejected by her pastor-turned-lover, JESSICA has enlisted her husband's coworker and love interest, MOLLY, for moral support on a trip to the abortion clinic. Here, as the women are getting to know each other, JESSICA explains why she has always been superstitious and in the process reveals her deep-seated dread of being alone.

JESSICA   The day it came out Meg Ryan and Dennis Quaid were splitting up, I saw something about it on a hospital TV, and it was just weirdly devastating to me, and I thought, This has to be a horrible omen. Otherwise I wouldn't feel so bad about it. And then my mom died later that afternoon, and ever since then I've been like a crazy person . . . You know what's always scared me? I'm not saying my dad flew off into somebody else's arms right away; he didn't. But right after she died . . . Sorry for telling you this; I'm in a weird mood . . . But after she died, all these middle-aged women started just . . . coming out of the woodwork, throwing themselves at him. I'd see it at church and my aunts' and uncles' parties. And I got to know a handful of them when he started dating, and they were all just so desperate. None of them were attractive, they had this . . . shellacked hair, and I remember thinking, Honey, you know not to use that much hair spray! I know you know that; have you not seen a magazine in twenty years!? What's happened to you!? And they weren't far from our age now, Molly. One of them was thirty-three! And that's when I figured out . . . If it'd been the other way around—if, God forbid, my dad had died and my mom had been the one to survive, there wouldn't be any men lining up to marry her. She'd have been alone for the rest of her life, just getting fat and doing ridiculous shit to her hair.

THE DRUNKEN CITY
Adam Bock

Seriocomic
LINDA, 20s

LINDA is a theology student, and in this direct audience address she describes how she feels when she goes into the "drunken city."

LINDA   I've been reading about Hinduism at school. The Hindus They think They think the whole world is alive That everything That every flower every bit of wood and rock and the floating clouds And even the water that a small golden fish swims through Everything is living and feeling And that night I believed them I could see the world that they I could see the city slowly opening its lazy dangerous eyes They The Hindus They use their breath to slow down the tumbling hurdy-gurdy of the world Slow it down so they can see the trees breathe, so they can fall in love with the wind, so they can That night I could hear it I could hear the cement under my feet muttering, I could hear the streetlights arguing with me, I could hear a devil and an angel struggling grabbing at each other, young and old and dead And I knew no one liked me and I knew and then I was dizzy and then I was fine.

THE DRUNKEN CITY
Adam Bock

Seriocomic
MELISSA, 20s

In this direct audience address, MELISSA *tells of her thrill at being proposed to by her fiancé,* JASON, *and then her deep despair when she realizes she has to break off the engagement because she finds out he has cheated on her with a girl named Jessica.*

MELISSA   This is how things get ruined. This is how things unravel and fall apart. This is how all of a sudden no one's smiling any more, why people end up standing around embarrassed and sad. I had everything. I had a ring. It was such a beautiful night the night Jason gave it to me. My hair was up like. And Jason looked so shiny and redfaced and he was smiling at me like I was the only person anywhere anywhere anywhere. It was gonna be awesome. And. And we were going to buy a house. I'd already picked it out. It had a gazebo in the backyard. With screens. Where you could put a table in the summer. Then slowly. Like a murmur that I didn't notice at first I couldn't hear it properly I kept hearing these two names. These two names over and over in different low voices. Jason and Jessica. Jessica and Jason. What kind of name is Jessica anyways. Who'd name their kid that? Jessica. It's a stupid name. It was humiliating. I gave my ring back to Jason. And suddenly all over again I had nothing all over again.

THE DRUNKEN CITY
Adam Bock

Seriocomic
MARNIE, 20s

MARNIE, the heroine of the play, is talking to FRANK, a man who is not her fiancé, who she has accidentally kissed during her bachelorette partying in the city. They are in a church, and she is trying to understand why she agreed to marry her fiancé, GARY, and coming to the realization that she can't marry him.

MARNIE   You gotta help me figure this out. Please? I wanted the wedding. Because it's gonna be a gorgeous wedding. I'm gonna wear my mom's wedding dress . . . it's from 1910 and her mom wore it and her mom's mom wore it and it's satin with inlaid pearls, well not inlaid pearls, that's not the word I'm, and I remember when I was a tiny girl I remember thinking "I gonna wear that dress" because it's the most, it's gorgeous and I'm gonna get to be looked at, I'm gonna, Gary was just a prop. He was. He was just . . . And I knew he wanted me to say yes, so I did. I just I kept lying . . . And then, worse, Frank, worse, he suddenly he he changed on me. He started acting like a husband. How he thinks a husband is, the world's dangerous and he has to protect me and that means I have to listen to him and he's gonna tell me what to do and I'm gonna have to act like he tells me. He's gonna be like his dad. But his mom's this little mousy woman who never says boo. And I'm not gonna be her. Uh-uh. But I just don't know what to say to Gary. I want to tell him the truth. I do. It's good you brought me here. I'm gonna need some help doing all this. Will you wait for me? I'm gonna go sit and be quiet for a minute. You're so sweet. I wish I'd met you before I met Gary.

ELECTRA

Don Nigro

Seriocomic
LEXIE, 28

LEXIE RYAN *is smart and attractive, with a quick mind and a dark sense of humor. She is the middle child of* CAROLYN *and the late* MICHAEL RYAN, *a banker. Her older sister* JENNA *is in the madhouse for killing their father in the bathtub with a pair of scissors while she was giving him a haircut, but* LEXIE *is convinced that in fact their mother* CAROLYN *killed him for the insurance money, then blamed it on her already mentally troubled daughter. Their younger brother,* THOMAS, *long believed to be dead, is just back from the First World War, and is deeply, deeply traumatized by his experiences there.* LEXIE *has taken him to the cemetery to visit their father's grave. She is trying to work up the courage to reveal to him the truth about her father's death, and to convince him to help her murder their mother and her lover* NICK.

LEXIE   There it is. That little mound of earth, under the wild cherry tree. They still haven't put the stone up. The man who does the tombstones caught his wife in bed with a Bible salesman and tried to carve a derogatory inscription on her backside and in the ruckus they knocked over a candle and set the house on fire, and the Bible salesman burned to death hiding in the fruit cellar, so the tombstone carver's in jail for manslaughter, and our father's grave is still just marked by a little pile of dirt. That's the sort of thing that happens around here. Dark, low comedy. Mother ordered a megalith the size of Stonehenge to impress the neighbors, but almost nobody speaks to us now. People stare at us on the street and mutter at each other like extras in a bad Greek chorus. Mother used to enjoy so much wringing her hands and wailing over and over, "My son is dead, my son is dead." She likes to hear the sound of her own voice so it drowns out any attempt to think on her part or anybody else's. But here you are, and it's Papa who's dead. I still can't believe you're here. But everything seems like a dream now. Even the birds are strange since he died. I don't like the way they look at me. There's something wrong with the crows. I wake up in the morning and everything seems just slightly out of place. I look at the trees and think, "Did somebody move them over night? Do the trees walk around all night and then never quite get back in exactly the right places?" Everything here is Through the Looking-Glass. I wonder where Loopy Rye is today. You know things are bad when the village idiot is ashamed to be seen with you. It's going to rain again. It always rains now. God, I hate monologues. Please say something so I can shut the hell up.

EXQUISITE POTENTIAL
Stephen Kaplan

Seriocomic
LAURA, early 30s

LAURA*'s husband* ALAN *thinks their 3-year-old son,* DAVID*, is the Messiah.*

LAURA   Even if he is the Messiah, we can't tell him. We can't tell anybody. We have to keep it a secret. Alan—if you love me. If you love David. If you love our unborn child—we will not talk about this again. It's not a question of if I believe you or not. But I will not talk about it again. It's too big for me. I will support you and I will help you and I will help our son and I will help our daughter and I will open myself up to the possibility of this, but I cannot talk about it again. Ever. Please. That's not saying whether it's true or not true, it's just saying that this is the end of it. Out loud. Never. OK? We love him. We don't treat him any differently. We do what we did when we brought him here today—go through our routine—and if he's the Messiah then there's nothing we can do that will stop that. Look, I don't know much about the New Testament, but Mary and Joseph didn't really have that much to do with Jesus's path to Messiah-hood, did they? I mean there's no talk about anything different they did with him than they would have with any other child. They taught him to be a good person—to be caring, to be loving, to treat people with respect, to stand up for himself, to think freely—aren't we already doing the same things for David? The only way we're going to screw him up is if you tell him that you think he's the Messiah. Nobody can live up to that. Even if they are the Messiah. We teach him that he is but dust and ashes and also that for his sake the world was created.

THE FALLEN
Yasmine Beverly Rana

Dramatic
SABINE, mid-30s

It is summer of 2008 in Trieste, Italy, and SABINE, *a Bosnian tourist, has just spent the night in a hotel room with* ANDREJ, *a fisherman formerly of Bosnia.* SABINE *questions* ANDREJ's *role during their country's conflict.*

SABINE   What did you do during the war? It was awful wasn't it? Sometimes I don't feel like being a nurse anymore, because I remember what I had seen, even today, even if my patient today will have a happy ending. It's hard to be so happy, but we have to, right, despite what we saw. And what did you see? I saw women, girls, some I knew, jump from the apartment buildings, those buildings you may have helped build, before the war, those buildings whose insides were blown apart, but whose roofs were amazingly intact, as if left, as a gift, to us, to find a way . . . to finish . . . what you had started, to end us. I saw the eyes of the women I performed abortions on, in the shelters of those bombed out roofless buildings, those raped and held and forced to be pregnant. I would walk, no, run. Run for my life, across the boulevards, through the roof-less buildings, down the stairs, the broken stairs, into the shelters. I would say that too. "I don't see this. I don't hear it. I don't feel it. I'll do what I have to do to help those who need me, but I'm not one of them. I won't allow myself to be a part of this. A part of them." Is that how you survived? By forgetting you were . . . a part of them, but not a part of us. Us, being . . . the other? What did you see? But every-one was doing it, right? Wearing a uniform. Wearing a ski mask over your face to hide, or perhaps to mask what you were truly feeling. You had to join the army, right? Become a nationalist? Hate us? Rape us? Kill us? What are you afraid of? Killing me now that you're finished and tossing me into the Adriatic Sea?

THE FARM
Walt McGough

Dramatic
PARKER: 20s–30s, African American

A new operative at the CIA, PARKER *has been charged with interviewing a retiring agent, and discovering what went wrong on his final mission. The agent is not cooperating.*

PARKER   Let me explain something to you. The Farm is for convalescence. The Farm is the finish line. The Farm is really fucking far away from you right now, because you've spent the last twenty-four years maintaining the ability and willingness to kill anyone you encounter, and that's a very useful thing for fieldwork, but not for a retiree, no matter how much government-funded beer he drinks at some resort. Does that make sense? You are not unique. You are not special. You are a tool, that was mass-produced two decades ago to be a very specific way, and all of a sudden you decided you didn't want to be a tool anymore, and you walked away from it, and that decision happened to come shortly after a mission that you pretty much have to agree went to fuckshit with no warning. There are a lot of red flags there. I've read your resignation, and I've watched the debriefings, all of them, and I've heard all the song-and-dance about "the way things was," and the only thing that I have gotten out of all that is the impression that you are a man who is trained to lie to people, and you are incredibly good at your job. And, you are using all of your considerable faculties in that department to pretend to be balanced, and stable, and ready for reentry into society. I don't buy it. Something went wrong, something that you're trying to keep down, and you think it's okay and that you can just keep it inside and go into the real world with it, but it's not okay because you don't know how the real world works anymore, and you haven't for two decades. And that means that I am going to keep you in this goddamn room until you've convinced me that you're not going to flip out at a Costco and choke a toddler because you think that he's wearing a wire. Once I'm satisfied, you can go to the Farm, but the burden of proof is on you.

THE FARM
Walt McGough

Dramatic
PARKER: 20s–30s, African American

PARKER *is a new operative at the CIA, having come to Langley after dropping out of training to be a Secret Service agent. After being goaded by the agent she is interrogating, she explains why she decided to change jobs.*

PARKER   I didn't get fired from the Service. I quit.

[*Beat.*]

> You heard of the dead man's twenty seconds? It's the amount of time you have to live, on average, if you get shot in the femoral artery. If you're in the service, if you're training, like I was, then your instructors all tell you to spend that time shooting. Because you have something bigger than you to protect. You have the President. And he's your life. If someone runs at him, you step in the way. If the plane's crashing, you give him your chute. If anything goes wrong, you always know just where he is. Always, always, always. And if a firefight starts, and you take one in the leg? Twenty seconds. Keep on shooting. Protect him. You spend whatever time you have left getting out in front, and when you're finally dead they use your body as a shield. I never really got that. It didn't . . . I don't know. Click. I aced all of the tests, I hit whoever I had to, I was fit, but when the time came down to it, and it was the package or me, I . . . hesitated. I got a lot of fake presidents killed. And I felt like I was failing. Like I was a bad soldier, whatever. So one day, I finally have a break, and I go out for a walk. And it's cold, it's icy, and coming towards me, there's this woman. She's

pregnant. Fifty feet in front of me, her stomach is . . . she must have twins, or triplets, she is *huge*. And she's coming towards me, and all of a sudden, she slips. Hits an ice patch, and just goes down, face first. And I'm too far away, I can't stop her, but she . . . she throws out her arms, right out in front, and she's falling *hard*. And she throws out her arms, and her hands hit the ground, right on her palms, and she pivots a little, and crumples. I get over to her. She's on her side. I roll her over, and I look down at her hands, and her wrists are both broken. Compound fractures. And her hands hanging there, her arms are both limp, and she's looking at me, saying, "Oh my God, I hurt the baby." Over and over. Now, she didn't. Hurt the baby. Her stomach never touched, she caught herself, with her hands, and then rolled, but she . . . I call an ambulance, and stay with her the whole time, and all she talks about is this baby, how she's scared that she hurt it when she obviously didn't. All she says. And that's what they want you to do, in the Service, and I don't have it. Whatever it is, that makes you throw out your hands? I can't see myself doing that for something *inside* of me, let alone . . . So I quit. And my instructor recommended me to Wilcox. Said they were recruiting, big time, and they could probably use someone like me. Whatever that meant. And so I went, and joined up, and then in training I read all your files, and I thought, well, yeah. Maybe. They could probably use someone like me. So? Did I tell the truth?

FIX ME, JESUS
Helen Sneed

Seriocomic
ANNABELL, late 20s to early 30s

ANNABELL *is campaigning on behalf of a Democratic gubernatorial candidate in Texas who has little chance of winning because his opponent's name is* DAVID CROCKETT. *She is speaking from the pulpit of an African American church, asking them to vote for her candidate, who defeated an African American in the primary.*

ANNABELL   I . . . I am . . . I stand . . . You may have noticed there's a white person standing up here in your pulpit in your church. It's amazing how white people just love to go to black church at election time. Well, Reverend Jefferson took pity on me and let me come before you today. We're in trouble. There's an election on and I can't get a single Democrat in Dallas to care. If things don't change, I'm going to die of loneliness on November 5, or get trampled to death by all those white people rushing to vote for Davy Crockett. I work for your candidate, a fine man named Walter Mapp. And yes, that's why I'm here: to convince you to vote for him and the Democratic ticket. [*Pauses.*] Look. This is the umpteenth time a white person has come across town to ask for your vote. My father's come to you before, and now it's my turn. But this year, something's different. I'm embarrassed because I'm here to ask you to compromise. You had a supremely qualified candidate and I wish we were one week out from electing Brenda Hawk the first black governor of Texas. But we're not. We didn't get our first choice. Everyone's saying both candidates are mediocre, the evil of two lessers. [*Pauses.*] How to explain this? My grandmother passed away last Sunday. She was eighty-four and had a long, vigorous life. She was quite a character—slept with a pearl-handled .22 pistol under her pillow because the Communists were coming. She was fierce. Hated the Russians, the Jews, the Chinese, the Catholics, gays, white trash, and uppity women. And boy, did she hate all of you. Didn't like me much, either. But. Last week, as she lay dying, she made one last demand. She insisted on voting absentee. We held her up to sign the ballot. Yes, my grandmother voted for every right-wing nut on the ticket, and yes, she fought all the wrong battles, but she kept fighting until the minute she died. There's courage in that and I'm asking you to do the same. We can't stop fighting just because we didn't get our way. And we must take moral action, even when our hearts aren't in it. If we stay home, we lose. Besides, someone in this church needs to cancel out my grandmother's vote. On Election Day, your grandmother is exactly as powerful as mine. November 5 may be the only day of pure justice coming your way. Don't you dare miss it. Vote for Walter Mapp. Vote Democratic. Vote for your grandmother, your children, yourself. Close your eyes and pretend it's for Barbara Jordan if you have to! Look. Ronald Reagan has turned America from a nation that *does* good into a nation that *feels* good. We Democrats must do better. The Republicans have plucked this thin-lipped white boy out of West Texas, where there aren't any black people—and just because his name is Davy Crockett, every white person in Texas is going to vote for him. Well, the original Davy Crockett was just some redneck cracker from Tennessee who was dumb enough to get killed at the Alamo. Why on earth would we want to elect another one? People of color brought down the first Davy Crockett. You can defeat this one, too. "Remember the Alamo" will have a whole new meaning. Thank you. God bless you. Remember the Alamo!

A GIRL'S GUIDE TO COFFEE
Eric Coble

Comic
ALEX, 23

ALEX *is a "barista extraordinaire." This is her own personal Seven Ages of Man speech.*

[*To audience.*]

ALEX   A trap: The Seven Ages of Remote Control Man. At first the infant—it doesn't matter what they put in front of you—purple dinosaurs, talking animals, puffy clouds—as long as it moves, blinks and makes noise, it's good television. And you have NO control over the remote. Then the school kid—it's the battle between your little superego and your little id: PBS numbers and letters vs. Cartoon Network hammer hits and booger jokes. And your parents tend to have the remote. Then as you slide into puberty, you grab the control and it's reality shows, music videos, clothes, sex, music, sex, skin care, sex, slang, sex, sex, sex, sex, sex . . . and then POP, you're out into the working world and it's News and Wall Street Channels at the office by day, and by night it's sitcoms and crime dramas where you learn life lessons in twenty-two or forty-four minutes. Unless it's *American Idol*, where you learn your life lesson by having a bunch of fans who can text. And then some Comedy Central, late-night TV to bed. But you put on a few years, you find yourself drawn into your niche, your rut, your "lifestyle," your ESPN, your HGTV, C-SPAN, History Channel, Cooking Channel, until suddenly you're old. And you find yourself watching the Weather Channel—actually watching the Weather Channel as your default, or just having it on in the background because it's . . . comforting . . .

to know there's weather happening . . . somewhere . . .
And then the last stage of all, that ends this viewing history, is second childhood, where you'll stare at pretty much anything as long as it moves, blinks, and makes noise. And once again someone else has control of the remote. Don't let this happen to you.

A GIRL'S GUIDE TO COFFEE
Eric Coble

Comic
ALEX, 23

ALEX *tells us about the typical male denizens of coffee shops.*

[*To audience.*]

ALEX   Okay, right? Yes. He's cute. I know. Great. But that's about as big a trap as staring at the TV all night. They both encourage you to put down roots and stay and just . . . stare. But especially boys, cute boys, intriguing cute boys, intriguing cute boys who are artists and can think on their feet . . . they can be even more dangerous because if you get attached to them, you can screw the whole delicate ecosystem we've set up here.

[*Begins working as she talks.*]

See, the basic building blocks of life in a coffeehouse are the "In-and-Outs," the ones who know what they want, get it and go, constantly churning the air, the coffee, the baked goods. "In-and-Outs" come in a variety of specimens: the Hard Hats, the Chilled Cops, the Starving Students. It's easy to take these organisms for granted, but without that constant turning over, everything else dies. And without them you wouldn't get to the truly interesting species: for instance, the Recoverus Addicti— AA, heroin, cigs, you name it. You have the best chance of seeing them at dawn; they've already been up for hours and are just happy to have somewhere to go and someone to talk to. A lot. And an offshoot of this species is the Odiferous Coagulatoria, the five old guys camping out in the corner ordering nothing or next to nothing, because they can subsist on talk about communism, poetry, and how they'd fix the universe, which they'd stand a better chance of doing if they'd take the occasional shower. Your dilemma with them is, are you sympathetic and let them grow, or businesslike and weed 'em out? 'Cause they spread like kudzu. Communist philosopher kudzu. And they come into conflict with the Laptopus Americanus, recognizable by their businesswear, they come in and build nests, setting out whole workstations and commencing to create new worlds while ingesting upscale drinks and muffins.

They share the same markings as the Americanus Lonely, but the latter aren't on company time—they just write letters, do the crossword, read the newspaper—all things they could do at home, but at home they'd be alone. So they're here. And beside them are the Maternia Escapus—middle-aged females, the occasional male, who have dropped their offspring off . . . somewhere . . . and are now sharing news and mating rituals over lattes and teas. And flying above all this are the Biker Boyum, the couriers who dart in, grab a drink, scan the newspaper, and are out the door for a day of running words and objects to the larger world, carrying your cup, your brand, your seed out with them like bees with pollen drifting from their legs. And then you have the midges and gnats of the world: the Frat Boys and Sorority Sisters who tend to be visible only at night and on weekends, ordering French Vanilla Cappuccinos (which don't exist—French Vanilla is an ice cream, not a coffee), so you make them something lethal like a Chocolate Mocha or Caramel Cooler Machiatto, and they survive it because they haven't eaten in a week. But they all—the whole system—flows together, feeds on each other, builds and collapses a thousand times a day. And you can't start injecting new species or new relationships, no matter how cute the boy, because it really is . . . a perfectly balanced system . . .

H2O
Jane Martin

Dramatic
DEBORAH, 20s

When DEBORAH *arrived to audition for* JAKE'*s production of Hamlet, he had just slit his wrists. She called 911 and saved him. She has just learned that the production is to proceed, and she has been cast as Ophelia, even though she never auditioned.* JAKE, *a movie star, is a cynical who-gives-a-shit kind of man, for whom life is a meaningless, endless farce. Not for her.*

DEBORAH   I'm not in a farce, Jake. Sorry. I am in my life in God's service. I've been in New York for four years and I have done eleven Shakespeares in parks, and parking lots and prisons and an abandoned hospital and I have never gotten more than bus fare, so my story is a little different than yours. Until two months ago I lived with seventeen women in the dormitory of a Christian hostel. I have seventy dollars in checking and nine dollars in my bag. You think you're a joke? I won't do plays that don't enable God's handiwork . . . now let's see you make a career out of that? Oh, and I don't take handouts. You want an argument for the existence of God, try Shakespeare. He transcends man while showing what man could be. Which, by the way, Mr. Abadjian, you don't. So despite the fact I would commit . . . sins . . . to play opposite Dawnwalker, because everybody who is anybody will come to gawk at you, and I will blow them away and have an actual career that I can use to fill my heart and bring people to Christ. But I'm not going to demean my talent and purpose so you can feel better about your infinite confusion and wasteful life.

HARBOR

Chad Beguelin

Dramatic
DONNA, mid-30s

DONNA, *a sometime singer and full-time screwup, has shown up in Sag Harbor along with her teenaged daughter* LOTTIE *at the house of her brother* KEVIN *and his husband,* TED. DONNA *is homeless and she and* LOTTIE *live in a van.* KEVIN *is an aspiring novelist who is totally supported by* TED. *He has asked* DONNA *to read his manuscript. Here, she comments on it. And, by the way, she's pregnant again and wants* KEVIN *and* TED *to take her baby.*

DONNA   You wanna know why you're so blocked on your book? It's because you're afraid that if it isn't published, you're going to be forgotten. That's the problem. There's going to be no one around to remember you. Your story just ends. But when you have kids, you're immortal, Kevin. You're part of something eternal. Without that, what have you got? It's just you and Ted growing old in this scary museum of a house and then just dying someday with nobody caring. It's the saddest story ever told. I've known you much longer than Ted, and you've always wanted to be a father. Well, technically, you always wanted to be a mother, but from the looks of things around here, we're not far off. The point is, I'm worried about you, Kevin. You're going down a path that you never wanted to go down. Here's your chance to have your cake and eat it, too. Ted will understand. I've seen the way he looks at you. He loves you. And who knows? Maybe it'll give you something to write about. Wouldn't that be nice? And obviously it'll help me out. I mean, I can't raise another baby, look at how I fucked Lottie up six ways from Sunday. I'm in a bit of a panic here, too, you know. I can't be in a band with a baby. I can't sing on a cruise ship. So I'm just going to have to give it away anyway. You want your unborn niece to go to strangers?

HEADSTRONG

Patrick Link

Dramatic
SYLVIA: early to mid-30s, African-American

SYLVIA *is talking to her father, a retired star NFL lineman. SYLVIA's estranged husband RONNIE, a former star NFL running back, disappeared and, after many months of addled, wandering home-lessness, has recently been found dead, a suicide from drinking antifreeze. She has been asked by a man who works for an orga-nization that studies deceased football players in order to deter-mine the effects of football contact on their brains to sign papers consenting to allowing them to examine RONNIE's brain for signs of Chronic Traumatic Encephalopathy. Her father is adamantly opposed to cooperating with the man. SYLVIA was too—until she begins to wonder if her own father might be suffering from CTE.*

SYLVIA   You've given me three pairs of the same heels over the last three months. Now maybe that's just 'cause you love these shoes so much, but judging by your face I don't think that's the reason.

[*Beat.*]

I didn't want to say anything. I almost did, but . . . I tried to think that it was just an accident, just a coincidence, but then I realized . . . it's that you don't remember giving them to me. And that's when I signed and faxed the papers. You don't remember giving them to me. Three times? You put milk in the cabinet sometimes. Fresh milk. I put it back in the fridge. You leave the cap off. I put it back on. I clean up after you. I do the grocery shopping so you don't buy six bags of marshmallows. I hope you're just absentminded. I hope you're just getting old. I hope Ronnie just suffered depression for some unexplained, unconnected reason. That hitting his head against the ground and against other helmets ten or twenty thousand times had nothing to do with his downward spiral. But I know it did.

[*Beat.*]

Yes, football paid for this house and my ring and all three pairs of these shoes. But now we have to pay for football. And you might say that the only thing you care about is winning, but what's the point of winning if you can't remember that you won?

HOLOGRAM

Don Nigro

Dramatic
LAURA, 26

LAURA has just started graduate school and seems to be doing well, but in fact she is a troubled girl, abandoned by her parents, raised by her stepfather, STEPHEN, upon whom she's projected many contradictory but powerful feelings, including gratitude and love, but also anger at her parents and at him for not loving her enough, and also a deep undercurrent of suppressed erotic attachment, a feeling that STEPHEN shares but has been trying to fight. Here she has called him late at night and is ostensibly giving him ideas for the novel he's been writing, but in fact she's confronting him directly for the first time with the essence of their own situation. In the play, although it's presumably a phone call, no telephone is present or mimed. She is in a circle of light speaking to us as if directly to him.

LAURA   Suppose the daughter is in love with her stepfather. Suppose she's been waiting to grow up so she can take her mother's place. But it isn't just her. There's a kind of conspiracy between them. Between her and the stepfather. An unspoken conspiracy. They both know. They've known for years. But they never talk about it. But it's always there between them. It's perfect. See, that's what drives the mother out of her mind. That's why she goes away. She knows they want to get rid of her. That it's not really about her at all. It's about them. And so she gives them what they want. It's an act of love, really. Well, a demented act of love by a self-destructive crazy person, but then, what isn't? But wait. This is the good part. That's what they've both been secretly hoping, right? The daughter and the stepfather, that the mother will go away. So she goes away and gives them what they want, because she can't take it anymore and she's losing her mind or whatever, and the thing is, when she actually does go away, it totally freaks them out. To get what they wanted is terrifying. And also, they're both really hurt. That she would leave them. Because her being there is what's allowed them to have this mutual fantasy that they never talk about, the fantasy that when the girl grows up she's going to marry the stepfather. It was really exciting, as long as they didn't talk about it. But now that the mother is gone and it's just them all alone in that house the both of them are terrified out of their minds. Except the stepfather is even more terrified than the daughter. What do you think?

HOME OF THE GREAT PECAN
Stephen Bittrich

Comic
PRISCILLA, 18

Beauty queen front-runner and high school senior PRISCILLA ROTTWEILLER is practicing her acceptance speech in the mirror for the crowning as Seguin, Texas's Pecan Queen. Little does she know that soon her whole world will be thrown into horrible disarray when someone (or something) steals the symbol of the 102nd Annual Pecan Festival from the town square—namely, the five-hundred-pound statue of the Great Pecan.

PRISCILLA   Thank you. Thank you, one and all. I'd like to thank the members of the selection committee for this great honor. I am sure it could not have been an easy decision considering all of the intelligent, beautiful contenders for the crown—

[*As she nods to each of the losers.*]

—Tawnya Blackhorn, DeAndra Loogan, Cynthia Morales. Wonderful, wonderful competitors all. I pledge that I will wear the crown of Pecan Queen with pride and distinction for the year to come. No thank-you speech would be complete without thanking my dear, dear family—my baby brother, Deke; my father, head engineer of Structural Metals, Inc.—

[*Waving to Daddy.*]

Hi, Daddy. And lastly, but certainly not leastly, my mother, who, by example, has taught me the true meaning of womanhood—

[*Acknowledging a knock at the bathroom door, her angelic demeanor turns satanic.*]

WHAAAAAAAT! Oh for the love of God, Mother, just start dinner without me! I'm in the middle of my speech! I'll be down in a minute! *Comprende inglese?*

[*She lets loose a huge, painful sigh, as she tries to recompose that sweet, dutiful demeanor and remember where she left off in the speech.*]

Hi, Daddy. Hi, Daddy. Hi, Daddy. And lastly, but certainly not leastly, my mother, who by example has taught me the true meaning of womanhood. *Je t'aime, ma mere.* I think it was that wise philosopher, Camus, who said, "This is the dog's dick."

[*Beat.*]

Oh, my. Did I just say, "dick"? Mercy me. I have just said "dick" and turned you all into horny toads. Dick, dick, dick. Dog's dick.

[*Like she is doing a newsflash.*]

"Pecan Queen shocks the world—says 'dick' in front of an adoring crowd of onlookers." Now that I'm Pecan Queen, there are going to be a few changes around here. First of all, DeAndra Loogan, you will carry my train for the entire year—always following a respectful twenty-eight steps behind. I have a *very* long train. Where was I? Ah, yes, of course. This will be the year when the Pecan Queen makes a difference. This will be the year when the Pecan Queen takes some action—solves World Hunger. World Peace. And combats gaucherie in all its forms. This I promise.

HONKY

Greg Kalleres

Seriocomic
EMILIA: 30s, African American

EMILIA *is a black therapist. Her white patient,* PETER, *is consumed with guilt over a sneaker commercial he wrote that may have inspired the shooting of black kid. Until now,* EMILIA *she has struggled to repress all her racist thoughts toward him. But when* PETER *explodes, telling her he's sick of feeling guilt for being white,* EMILIA *can't take it anymore.*

EMILIA   And Charley Cross? Are you sorry for him too? That's funny. I thought that was the entire reason you were in therapy. A fourteen-year-old African American boy shot in the face because of a commercial.

[*Beat.*]

Imagine me listening to a man apologize over and over without the first clue as to what he's sorry for. He thinks it's because he's white. Well. Isn't that a shame? Even his contrition is out of context. His shame, ignorant and irresponsible.

[*Beat.*]

This was never therapy. It was a confession. To the only black person you know. And you thought if we went out, if you charmed me and we connected as people it would somehow magically pardon you of all wrongdoing. An instant hall pass that would walk you past every Negro you meet with a fist bump.

[*Beat.*]

I come in here every day and listen to the problems of white folks. Crackers with cracker problems and cracker guilt! I tell myself to be objective. Listen to the issues. Be understanding. "They're not white people," I say, "they're people with problems." But after a while it doesn't take. No matter how many pills I swallow, it doesn't suppress. But this is my job. To tolerate it. To pretend, like you, that I understand. That I don't seethe with my own disgust. My own shame. But the problem, Peter, is that I do understand. Your fortunate problems? I get it. I too am unscathed. Untouched. Like you. So, I donate to the NAACP and I volunteer to the United Negro College Fund. And I do it all to absolve myself. Ignorantly. Out of context. Just. Like. You. So, you see, you came to the wrong nigger for exoneration. You feel ashamed for your whiteness? So do I, Peter. So do I.

HOW WATER BEHAVES
Sherry Kramer

Comic
NAN, mid to late 20s

NAN *and her husband are going through a rough patch economically. She doesn't make much money and he just lost his job. To make matters worse,* NAN *was at a poetry reading and a thief stole her purse, containing all their Christmas money. The poet, a nice guy named* ALLEN, *found her purse, and brought it to her at home. When he asks where her husband is,* NAN, *not wanting* ALLEN *to think that her husband is a loser, makes this up.*

NAN   My husband? My husband is at work of course. He
works . . . he works for . . . a charitable organization. Like
the Bill and Melinda Gates Foundation, only smaller.
Much smaller. Of course, size isn't everything—it's the
work that matters. And my husband's charity does very
important work, it well . . . well . . . well . . . it digs wells!
His charity drills wells in Africa! It's called All's Well When
It Ends with a Well. It was started by theater people.
He makes almost . . . nothing, that's why losing all our
Christmas money is sort of a blow. We have this arrange-
ment—one of us has the money job, and the other one
has the repairing the world job. I got stuck with the money
job. The problem is, the money job doesn't actually make
very much. Money. I wish I had the repair of the world job.
When you work at a place like All's Well When It Ends with
a Well, or, say, the Bill and Melinda Gates Foundation, you
work with very evolved people. You work with people who
care about things, and I bet you can take as long a lunch as
you like, because your long lunches are with *other* people
who are also trying to repair the world . . . you're working to

make the world better during breakfast, lunch, and dinner, all the time . . . you're dedicated instead of driven, or rather, you're driven in the best way and it doesn't make you crazy or cranky when you come home from work. And it's always clear what's right and what's wrong, even though it's sometimes hard to see the best way to do the good, you are still clear about good. Everyone's fair and kind to each other, and everybody's ideas are given equal consideration. And nobody cares about things like fashion or pro-football or anything trivial, nobody in your office has a face-lift or gets Botox. All the paper is recycled effortlessly, the coffee in the coffee room is fair-trade organic, and it's always the right temperature without ever turning the heat or conditioning on. It's like a temple, a sacred place.

Sometimes, I imagine that I am Melinda Gates. I am wearing a white sari with patterns woven with gold threads in it and I am saving the world from malaria.

[*A sweeping gesture with her hand.*]

I just wave my hand and poof—the mosquitos are vaporized. I go to a leper colony—I hand out state-of-the-art pharmaceuticals Bill has cooked up in his spare time using a logarithm he found stuck on the bottom of his shoe while running a marathon to cure worldwide walleye. I walk through the streets of Bombay handing out Microsoft Word to infant programmers so they can pull their families out of poverty by the age of three. My hair blows in the breeze. I wear no makeup but I look refreshed and dewy at all times. I walk through the crowds like a good-looking Mother Theresa.

HOW WATER BEHAVES
Sherry Kramer

Dramatic
NAN, mid to late 20s

NAN *and her husband,* STEVE, *had a huge fight about the fake charity they invented—he wants to shut it down because it's ethically questionable, she wants to keep it going because it's becoming real and doing good work. At the end of the fight,* STEVE *walked out on her.* NAN *is terrified that her marriage is over, and she confides in her best friend,* MOLLY.

NAN
[*She gets a new pack of cigarettes out, unwraps it. Lights up.*]

This is my second pack. That's how I know this time it's bad. He's never stayed away a whole pack before. At first I smoked to punish him, because he hated it so much. Then I realized it was because I knew that by the second, or third cigarette, he'd be back. So it was a way to measure the time until he came home. But this time I keep smoking them, and he keeps not coming home, and . . . I just don't understand why he always has to behave a certain way because of some arbitrary rule book about right and wrong. Sometimes you have to bend the rules. I thought we wanted the same things. That we thought the same things were important. Now I walk in the house and I don't know where I am. Our whole life all of a sudden makes no sense.

[*She takes a big drag on the cigarette.*]

When I was little I went to a fun house called Confusion Hill. It was in this dying amusement park in the hills of Appalachia . . . everything was made out of fake rotten-looking wood that was so decayed it put real rotten wood to shame. When you stepped into Confusion Hill, everything was wrong. Big things looked small and small things looked big. Shadows were the wrong shade. If you dropped five balls on the floor, they attacked each other and then rolled away in five different directions at once. And best of all—water ran up hill. That's the thing that had me hypnotized. It was late, my parents were screaming my name, they thought I had fallen off a cliff or something, my sisters and brother were already loaded up in the car. But I wasn't going anywhere. I couldn't stop watching the water cascade into this trough and run uphill. Of course it was just an illusion. Gravity is the fundamental force in the universe. Without it everything we believe to be true just stops. Stops being true, and then, stops being. As long as gravity is stronger than water is, water has to behave. He's too much like water. His relationship with gravity is set. I can't change it.

HOW WATER BEHAVES
Sherry Kramer

Comic
NAN, late 20s to early 30s

NAN *and her husband* STEVE *are having a tough time of it economically (who isn't?). She's obsessed with the Bill and Melinda Gates Foundation, and she is ready to do anything to make her dream of donating money they don't have to save the world come true.*

NAN   Let's face it. We're a nation of parvenus. Social climbers. Arrivistas. The problem is that the entire middle class *has* arrived, and it doesn't make us feel as good as we thought it would. Money has not made us happy. Even the 1 per-centers aren't happy. Money doesn't work the way it used to. You walk down the street, can you tell who's 1 percent and who isn't? No. You can't. No matter how rich you are, you can't have a better iPhone than the guy who serves you at MacDonald's. It doesn't exist. And when it does exist, next month it will come out for $199.99. So you're in the 1 percent and you have seven luxury vacation homes. But everything you have in those houses is probably in half of the houses of the 99 percent—do you know what this Mac, with this much computing power, would have cost if it existed twenty-five years ago? Like 2 million dollars? Now you can get a less elegant iteration for a couple of hundred bucks. You can get better face-lifts when you're rich, and private jets are nice. Bigger diamonds on your fingers, cars that give other cars inferiority complexes. But your life isn't better the way it used to be better, it isn't separate and all gold leafed—you're rubbing elbows with the riff-raff everywhere you go. Everybody has what you have, either the real McCoy or the knockoff version, and if their knockoff makes their life better the way your real one does, then what's the difference between you and them anymore? There's no way to be really rich except philanthropically. That is their Alamo. Their final stand. The philanthropic buzz of Palm Beach is the last real thing they had. So of course I wanted to have it.

JESUS IN INDIA
Lloyd Suh

Dramatic
ABIGAIL, late teens

ABIGAIL *and* JESUS *travelled to India together. She loves him, but he dumped her so she went back home to Galilee. Now she has returned, with a plea to him to return home with her.*

ABIGAIL   Your father's died. Your father's dead, Jesus. Joseph is dead. Murdered. It's all such a mess, back home— there's hardly home left. It's war. Herod is dead and there is no order, the Romans have overrun everything, and they won't stop until they've completely eliminated every single Jew from the face of the Earth. But there's a resistance. We've fought, we fight, your mother and I, along with others. I would have come sooner but every pair of hands is needed, there are so few working on behalf of the Jews. I came because we need you. Your father wasn't a fighter. He wasn't a zealot, didn't cause any trouble. He was just there. You know. He was just a man. And they cut him down anyway, like they cut down many who are just men. Your people are dying, Jesus. We are fighting. And we are losing. We are dying. Your mother, she told me everything. About what your father said, about who you are, about what you're supposed to do, and I believe it, Jesus. I believe in you. You can build a house. You can build a table. But that's not what we need from you. We need you to build an army. We need you to build a revolution. We need you to build someplace for all these departed souls to go, to find some peace, somewhere your father and all our other fallen family can rest, because there are too many such souls now waiting in the streets

and gutters and mass graves of Galilee. Jesus. Please.
Build that shit. And I will follow.

It's time. Let's go home.

JIHAD JONES AND THE KALASHNIKOV BABES
Yussef El Guindi

Comic
CASSANDRA, 20s–30s

CASSANDRA *is an actress in a movie that is nothing but a mass of anti-Muslim clichés. She doesn't care and she's miffed that her costar,* ASHRAF, *does. He has principles—she doesn't.*

CASSANDRA   So you're miffed you're not playing a boffo character with a great personality and charm to spare. Well, boo-hoo. My pussy weeps for you. Excuse me while I break out the tissues for another struggling actor asked to play shit and make it real. What the hell kind of business do you think this is? An academy for the study of human behavior? This is the land of gummy bears and popcorn, and making out in the back row and leaving a mess for the ushers to clean up. It ain't deep; it's not real, and if you're lucky you get paid a whole lot. Shove it. I don't want to hear it. Save it for after I leave. Do you think I got to where I am today because I was picky? I'm *a woman*. Do you know what I get offered as *a woman*? In a business that prizes eye candy before everything else? Boobs and ass before character and content? Honey: the pickings are slim. I get my choice of whores, skanks, saints, or virgins. And that's when I'm not being offered whores, skanks, saints, or virgins. Or bitches. Or warrior princesses with penis envy. Or any combination of the above. The trough is full of swill, hon, and always has been, and if you're lucky you find one or two great nuggets in your career and that's what you live off while you forage through more trash. Stereotypes, please. You don't know anything about stereotypes till you've walked in my hooker boots for six weeks on a movie set. Get over it. I know my part isn't great. But I'm going to give it everything I have and make those pimply kids in the back row stop tonguing for two minutes and give me their full sex-crazed attention because goddamn it I deserve it. And if you've got any balls, you'll take this part and do the same. Jesus. You're an actor. Act like one, you little pissant. You all think on that while I go make some calls. And when I get back, if you're not finished agonizing over whatever it is you've got your boxers in a twist about, then—I'm gone.

LAST FIRST KISS
Chad Beckim

Dramatic
GABBY, 19

GABBY *has been crying her eyes out in the ladies room because she has just seen her prom date,* PETER, *kissing another boy. Now she knows why he's different from other boys—and why she loves him.*

GABBY   Every day, I see these girls—pretty girls, smart girls, like my friends, my sisters, their friends—all these girls surrounded by these stupid, selfish, asshole boys. I see all of these girls get treated like shit every single day, and just, take it. Day in, day out, just take this bullshit nonsense. And every day it made me more and more determined not to be like that. Me, thinking, "No way that's going to happen to me." Like, absolutely determined not to fall into that stupid boy trap, thinking, no way am I planning my free time and weekends and life around these stupid boys. I have spent a great deal of time avoiding these situations, because I see. I see that it's not permanent, that these guys just run around and try to say the right things and do the right things trying to, whatever, make out or cop a feel or get in your pants and all that. And I'm like, Not Me. No way. [*Beat.*] And then you. You come along and don't push. You're sweet. You're smart. Funny. You can hold a conversation that's not about video games or sports. You notice when I'm wearing something different. When I get my hair cut or wear it a different way. You like, respect me and treat me nice and . . . God this sounds so stupid. It's so different than anything I've ever seen from anyone else. I have never seen anyone else get treated the way you have treated me. So, I, whatever, let you in? I let you in. And now . . . now I randomly catch you kissing Tommy Miller in the chem lab. [*Beat.*] So you're gay. Whatever. That's fine. I feel stupid that I was too naïve to catch on before, but okay, whatever. Proms are supposed to be momentous occasions. This has certainly been a momentous occasion. [*Beat. She turns to him, direct.*] But I have to suspect that you knew about this long before I did. I don't believe that this was some, what, random, freak occurrence. So what was I to you? Huh? Was I, like, some sort of experiment? Some like, barometer for heterosexuality? A human litmus test? And don't try to hide behind some stupid bullshit excuse, because if you do I'll come over there and take that stupid flower off your lapel and stab you in the ear with it. Because if you were—and I have to believe that you were because you can't seem to even attempt to placate me with some semblance of an excuse—if you were using me as some test, that makes you slime. Because you knew. And you used me. And that makes you worse than any dumb guy, worse than slime. That makes you shit. [*Beat.*] So look at me. Look at me and promise me that you weren't using me like that.

THE LAST SEDER

Jennifer Maisel

Comic
MICHELLE, late 20s–early 30s

Fed up with her family's constant carping about her failure to bring a significant other to their annual seder, MICHELLE *approaches a total stranger and asks him if he will be her date this year. This is the "last seder," because the family patriarch is dying.*

MICHELLE   Ummm, excuse me—hi?—look, I know you don't know me, but you look like someone who might . . . might be open to a complete stranger asking you . . . I'm not some psychochick, in case you're thinking I am, which I'm sure you are—here's my license, so you know I'm me . . .

[*She hands him card after card from her wallet.*]

Here . . . library card, museum membership, prescription card—so at least you know I'm a semicultured literate insured psycho, I guess. Thank you for not running away. It's just that for months I've known this was coming, there's been this impending dread which was only exacerbated by the Hallmark store across from me—its windows a mad succession of hoblins, goblins, witches, and candy accented by Happy Jewish New Year and Day of Atonement cards, and Halloween wasn't even over before they added Indians and Pilgrims decorating Christmas trees sprouting out of Plymouth Rock, of which I doubt the historical accuracy, and then Valentine's Day, hearts everywhere since New Year's and now they have Easter Barbie . . . Easter Barbie for Christ's sake, which really gets me up in arms even though I'm not religious. Really, it's more of a cultural thing I have to admit, but all they'd have to do is stick a jar of gefilte fish and a Haggadah in the leftover Easter Barbies' hands and we'd make all the little girls with mezuzahs on their Malibu dream houses very—

[*She catches herself in the rant.*]

. . . happy. . . . Right. Well . . . every day . . . every day some relative calls me to confirm whether I'm bringing flourless chocolate cake this year to seder—with my family Passover is a big hullabaloo—not so much in a do-everything-according-to-the-rules sense, but more in a digging-horribly-and-obsessively-into-every-detail-of-your-life-between-appetizers-and-desserts sense—and since it's the last time . . . well . . . it's all much more . . . that. But they're really not calling to find out what I'm bringing, but who I'm bringing, and I couldn't put up with hearing Aunt Mabel say, "So Michelle, why don't you have a man yet?" in her frog voice. Again. I'm tired of making excuses and I'm tired of sympathetic "I've-got-a-friend"s. And this, this is the last year, so it becomes important in a way I can't explain. So I'm walking up to you, and you must think I'm crazy and I know you don't know me but you're wearing a nice suit and you looked somehow . . . right . . . and that's a step in the right direction anyhow. Do you like matzah?

LIDLESS
Frances Ya-Chu Cowhig

Dramatic
ALICE, 25

ALICE *in an interrogator at Guantánamo Bay prison. She is using a tactic called "invasion of space by a female," in which the threat of female sexuality is used to break down a Muslim man suspected of being a terrorist.*

ALICE   Hey now. For a second there, with the light on you like that, you looked like my Lucas. Call me overworked and underfucked, but from where I'm standing, y'all could be cousins [*Beat.*]. I'm touching myself. My fingers trail up my thigh as I think of all our bodies could do. I could sink into your hard, hot cock. I could bury my face in your neck. You could hold me. You could move me. You could help me find light and redemption and peace. What's the matter, Mo? Is the great Islamic sword too weary to rise today? [*Beat.*] Holy Mother. Looks like I found your sweet spot. Right here. An inch beneath your left ear. Jesus, I could hang Old Glory on that pole. I've been wasting my time on white boys. It appears those rumors about Asian men are lies your ladies tell to keep you to themselves. Selfish bitches. Now. What are we going to do about that boner?

[*She flinches and wipes invisible spit off her face.*]

Now, now. The only spittin' allowed is the kind that comes from down there. Besides. You like this. Our heads hearts try to trick us, but our bodies never lie. Roll with me, baby. Don't fight. Give it up, sweet pea. Stop your prayin'. If Allah was in Gitmo, we'd have him in solitary, so he wouldn't be able to hear you anyway. [*Beat.*] I forgot to tell you.

I'm bleeding, and there's nothing shielding you from my twenty-five-year-old cunt, just red, red, red, stainin' skin already caked pus white and blue with bruises, making you the color of the flag I've sworn to protect. I've read about your hell. Your silence condemns you to that furnace fueled by the flesh of men, where walls are fire, smoke's the only shade, and the only beverage is the blood bubbling though your veins, so you better hope to Allah there's no such thing as eternity.

[*She takes off her shirt, revealing a lacy push-up bra.*]

Last chance.

LIVE BROADCAST
John William Schiffbauer

Dramatic
MADDIE, early to mid-30s

MADDIE is a liberal congresswoman. She is appearing on a TV talk show, where she is debating a star actor who has conservative political views.

MADDIE   Have either of you ever been a witness to the actions of a gang or a mob? No? Then imagine for the moment that you're a sixteen-year-old girl. Five foot three, ninety-five pounds. You're good in school, but you can't be too good because guys don't like girls that are smart, or at least just not girls that are smarter than they are. You work a job after school to help save money to pay for your college books and tuition. You have a boyfriend that loves you, but has begun pressuring you to be more physically intimate with him. Your family is Roman Catholic. You've always been taught that God won't love you if you have sex before you're married, that your parents won't love you if you have sex before you're married, that no one will love you if you have sex before you're married. You will be cast out of the village for committing the crime of having premarital sex. But at the same time, you love your boyfriend and you know that he loves you. You want to be more physically intimate. You ask yourself, who am I hurting, in the end, who am I hurting if my boyfriend and I are more physically intimate with each other? So, one night, you agree to go out with him in his convertible. He drives you out to a hillside overlooking the town, and there under the cover of starlight and moonlight, the car radio acting as your own personal Maurice Chevalier, you find that you're both each succumbing to your basic human desires. Then you wake up a month later and discover you're pregnant, but it's okay because it's not like your family's that religious, right? No, wait, I misspoke—they're very Roman Catholic. So, what do you do? Well, first you tell your mother, who tells your father, who turns around and decides to rip you a new one. You little whore, he says, how could you have been so unbelievably stupid, how could you have allowed yourself to be taken in by this lying, self-serving, predatory fraction of a man? So, now that you feel like the lowest of the low, after you feel like you've betrayed your parents, your boyfriend, and Jesus Christ himself. Now that all you want to do is go into your room and slit your wrists with a razor, you realize you can't because there's a tiny little organism that has begun to grow inside of you. You are now responsible for what happens to this tiny little organism. You have the option of keeping it, of helping it grow to a full and healthy lifespan. Or you can get rid of it because you're sixteen, you can't support yourself let alone the needs of a newborn baby, and you want to go to college so you can get a job and move out from under the financial umbrella of your parents so that one day you might be able to do just that, to support the needs of a newborn baby. So, let's say you live in New York or Oregon, two states that do not require parental consent or notification to abort a pregnancy. You drive to the abortion clinic, but when you get there you see a mob of people standing between you and the front door holding signs and shouting things that make you want to turn around and hide under your bed. But you can't. You have to be brave. The problem is, it's hard to be brave when you're five feet three inches and ninety-five pounds. So, very quietly and very slowly you get out of your car. You walk towards the front door of the building, trying hard to avoid the gaze of what feels like a hundred pairs of eyes, all of whom have just decided to make you the new focus of their rage and ignorance. What happens next? From out of nowhere someone's hand slaps you across the face. If you weren't feeling bad enough before, you sure as hell feel like crap now. All you can do is run and hope they don't catch you and rip you to pieces before you can get to the other side of the front door. Why does Congress need to make it illegal to protest outside abortion clinics in this country? Because women seeking abortions shouldn't be made to feel like criminals.

LUCY LOVES ME
Migdalia Cruz

Comic
LUCY: 25, Latina

LUCY is trapped in an apartment with her delusional mother. In this monologue, LUCY finally finds a friend/potential suitor in MILTON, to whom she speaks about her job delivering pizzas and other things she finds interesting and, perhaps, impressive, on their first date.

LUCY   I like my job. Other people might not like it, but I do. I get a kick out of the kids who come up to me with thirty-six cents for a slice. "Don't you know what century this is, kid?" I say. They don't have a clue. So I give it to them anyway. I don't care. Why should I care? They're just little kids . . . You know what else I like? I like it when they turn off the ovens and everybody goes racing home . . . That's when I whip out a bag of Twizzlers—I find licorice real relaxing, you know what I mean? It like gives you time to think because you gotta chew it so long. I come to some interesting ideas that way. I'm gonna write a book about that place some-day. One chapter is gonna be just about Twizzlers and the things it makes you think. Another one's gonna be about sex. It's something the way people carry on there. There was this one woman who used to come around all the time. We called her Blowjob Linda; she used to grab guys and take 'em into the toilet with her. They'd come out minutes later with their shirts out and their flies open, looking like something blown in out of a tropical storm. Anyway, that's Linda. I could write a whole chapter just about her. You know what I mean? She had style. Not too many people with that. Yeah . . . you see all types. I think that's why I like it so much. It's always in-ter-esting. I think so anyway. I don't know about anybody else.

[*Pause.*]

You know what else? I like talking people into buying things they don't know they want . . . Yeah, that's the best. Pizza with pineapple and anchovies. Man, some people are sooo stupid, they'll eat anything.

[*Pause.*]

Some people tell me I'm too old to be delivering pizzas, but isn't that who you would want delivering your pizza? Somebody older. Somebody responsible. You know how not getting a pizza you ordered could ruin your evening. You could be left there with nothing to eat. And then you would have to go out. That's what I save people from. From the streets. From seeing other people. From having other people see them. I'm a shield.

THE MAN UNDER
Paul Bomba

Dramatic
LISA, 26

LISA *is talking to* JEFF. *She is a strange woman who likes to jump on the subway track and lay down flat while a train passes over her.*

LISA   Well, I had a fantasy too. I dreamt of throwing myself on the tracks. And once I was with you, but you were some other guy with some other problem and he also looked into my eyes as he grabbed that pole. I reached out for him and he slipped away and took the leap. That leap that I've been somehow fucking preventing myself from taking for the last eight, nine years. It's in slow motion, the way he moved . . . This hauntingly beautiful dance where the soul vacates the body and a powerful negative force propels this empty, mobile husk. One step and . . . I tried not to watch . . . but I was compelled to. Coerced by those tortured green eyes that spoke wordless to me not six seconds before. Just that one step and he seemed to . . . to just float there, balanced in the air for just this hair of a time. Just long enough for me to see a flash—a flash of regret in his eyes. He was looking at me asking me why I wasn't ready to save him, and I didn't have the answer. I could only stare into the depths of someone who was making that most permanent mistake. And I just . . . Time starts again and there's a terrible sound, the train grinds to a screeching halt, and the conductor runs out, yelling, "MAN UNDER MAN UNDER MAN UNDER!" like him shouting louder and louder was gonna raise the dead. The blood was splattered all over the platform and I started to hate that . . . I could've helped. Reached out. But I was only able to watch as a horror unfolded in real time right in front of me . . . With those green eyes . . . After a moment, I reached down for this . . .

[*Takes off glove.*]

The other one, well, it was down there on the tracks, probably mangled and broken like the rest of him. But this was saved, and it fell at my feet, like some kind of offering. The damnedest things happen when the human body is obliterated at high speeds . . . Physics, you know? Gloves come off. [*Pause.*] So that's it, now you know. And now you know why I needed to save you, see? You'll never be the man under. I won't let it happen. Because I'm loving you and holding on. And we'll never be able to regret anything. Because we're in some kind of . . . Some kind . . . of love.

MISSED CONNECTION
Larke Schuldberg

Comic
EFFIE, late 20s

EFFIE *approaches a handsome stranger in a bar.*

EFFIE   So studies show that of all the countries in the world, American women are some of the worst at flirting. Or, like, approaching men, initiating contact, whatever. I didn't actually read the study, but I read about it online. I'm not really in the habit of reading scientific studies—I mean, maybe I should be, maybe that's like what's wrong with my life—but this study totally supports the argument that gender roles are culturally taught and are not biologically innate, which I totally believe. But it's really hard to go against years and years of cultural programing that aggressive women are easy and no one wants to marry the slut and that men enjoy the chase and you should play hard to get otherwise it's boring. As though men are cats with a piece of string. And I realize that's not really a metaphor that makes sense but whatever. Simile? Metaphor. Whatever. But just because something is hard doesn't mean you shouldn't work on it. Being good at being aggressive, I mean, generally speaking, not just, like, flirting. And I am trying. I'm getting better. I asked for a raise at work, finally, I should have asked for it like six months ago, and it was awful and horrible and goes against my nature both because I want everyone to like me but also because I'm not really sure I'm worth twelve dollars an hour, you know? But I did it and even though I thought I was going to vomit, it actually ended up really awesome. I mean I didn't get what I asked for, but I did get a raise and that's good, right? I mean, I'm half Jewish so you'd think I'd be good at negotiating, but I'm really, really not. When I bought my car I got so ripped off and I knew it, but I didn't say anything because I was embarrassed. Is that anti-Semitic? Is something still racism even if it's positive? Like saying mixed-race babies are cuter? Am I allowed to say that? Because it's true, you know. But what I was saying is that I'm working on it, being aggressive, or well not aggressive but like stating what I want and feeling entitled that I deserve what I want and anyway I think you're sort of cute. Well not sort of cute, actually cute. You are actually cute. And so I'm trying to do this thing where if I think someone is cute I go up and tell them and this is really terrifying and I would like to buy you a beer if you want or if you don't want you can take the compliment because it's true that you're cute and if you want a beer I will be sitting over there and oh my god I am so sorry I will leave.

THE MNEMONIST OF DUTCHESS COUNTY

Josh Koenigsberg

Dramatic
GINA, 30s

GINA *owns a bar frequented by college students. She is talking to* MILO, *a campus security guard who hangs out there.*

GINA   Well it looks like there might be some people interested in buying the bar. Those guys back there from the City? We've been talking for a couple of weeks. Technically I'm not supposed to say anything yet—but they just walked right in here the other day and made me an offer. I mean I guess every other place around here near the Hudson is getting bought and refurbished. Anyway I just want to take my money and get out of this dump. . . . It's just . . . I've been here too long, y'know? It's like you begin to notice things like how the only clear radio station plays the same nine oldie songs over and over again and how the only people around here are either college kids or trust-fund hippies, or . . . sports-obsessed meatheads. [*Beat.*] And I don't like the nights here. It's like, growing up around here I was always scared of the wind at night, y'know? There's such a particular howl it has. And it used to remind me of like ghosts and werewolves and, I don't know, just horror movie stuff. But then as I grew up, it started reminding me of other things. Much scarier things. Like . . . growing old I guess. And being alone. Just totally completely alone where you go out during the day and shop for groceries just so you can eat them by yourself at night while you watch these TV shows that are filled with images of a world you don't even belong to. But that you convince yourself you *do*. And you keep trying to remember what it was like to be there, cause you can't face the fact that you're totally isolated. Alienated from everything and just completely alone. And you just keep on passing the time, passively passing time. Until you're old. And your bones won't move. And then that's it, there's nothing left. There's just—and you never even . . .

[*She gets choked up. She takes a deep breath.*]

Sorry. Maybe I'm crazy. I just don't want to hear that howl anymore y'know? I wanna go someplace warm, where the sun sets late, and there are lots of people around and I don't have to drive all the time and I just never want to hear that howl again.

MR. BURNS, A POST-ELECTRIC PLAY
Anne Washburn

Dramatic
SUSANNAH, 20s–30s

SUSANNAH *is sitting around out in the woods with a small group of people who have survived the recent biological and nuclear catastrophe that has killed most of the population. She tells them about a man who tried to get fuel to the generator at a nuclear power plant to prevent it from a meltdown.*

SUSANNAH   He told me that he had gone to do it, he had, he was at a gas station, a mile and a half from the main entrance. It's this gorgeous fall day and he's siphoning off one of the tanks. He has containers. He has a dolly, or—what are those things, where it's a couple of planks, basically, on wheels like this . . .

[*She indicates dimension.*]

. . . and usually it has strips of carpeting on it? He's determined, he's totally set to go. And then he had a, he had a. A flash? A very vivid—just one of those, fantasies you have all of a sudden. He said he saw himself walking towards the plant and there's the reactor right above him, and up the little service roadway and he's at the shed, the the the service shed, and he busts at the lock until he busts it open. And he pictures this shed as being vast, shadowy, and at the end of it this huge hulking generator. And he steps into the shed and he's maneuvering the dolly inside when he realizes, that it's quiet. It's so quiet. He lowers the dolly and he almost can't bear it but he walks, all the way across the shed, his boots on the concrete floor. He's standing right in front of the silent generator and he reaches out, he touches it: it's cold, dead. He's too late. And his heart is pounding. And he has a flutter in his stomach which he thought, What is this, is this adrenaline? And he thinks: probably not. And this ache, starting up in his head. And he leaves the shed and the reactor . . . it's right there, right above him, half lit up by sunlight, And now he gets the first wave of nausea. He discovers he's shitting his pants. And. This is weird. He doesn't want the reactor to get to watch him die. So he starts off, back down the road. And he's thinking, all I want is to get around that curve up there. So I'm out of sight. Feets, just carry me that far. Feets don't fail me now. And this is the point where he snaps out of it. He's standing at the gas station, with his dolly, and six gas canisters he's scrounged from garages, and a few plastic tubs he found in restaurants. And he looks up the roadway leading to the plant. And he knows he can't do it. He drops the siphon. He walks away. He said: it's not knowing, that's the problem. He said: I think I just can't handle the dread.

NEW IN THE MOTHERHOOD
(from Motherhood Out Loud)
Lisa Loomer

Comic
ODD MOM, 20s–30s

A mom joins some other moms in the park. She's kind of an odd mom out. Not sarcastic . . . just a bit bewildered and wry. She's fine with the kid, easy . . . The rest of her new life she's still trying to figure out.

ODD MOM   Oh hi. This bench taken?

[*Sits.*]

Cool.

[*Sees son. Calls out, lightly.*]

Put it down, Harry. Down, babe. The tricycle is a means of *transportation*.

[*Laughs.*]

He's three. Everything's a penis.

[*She takes out a cigarette.*]

God, I hate the park. If anyone had told me I'd be sentenced to five to ten years in the *park* . . . I'd have stuck with a cat.

[*Re: cigarette.*]

Oh, this is clove by the way.

[*Takes a drag.*]

All right, it's not clove, but it's the park. See, the park for me is like . . . Dante's Purgatory. Not Dante's Inferno—that'd be exciting, you'd meet interesting people . . . But, I mean, day after day of whose turn is it on the swing? Couldn't we just let 'em duke it out? I mean, I used to go to an office . . . Like—in a building? I was a type A personality! Okay, B minus, but still . . .

[*Takes a drag; smiles.*]

Look, I know he's a boy, you gotta take 'em outside. They *will not* play Scrabble. They'll throw the pieces at the cat. And they won't miss, 'cause they're boys.

[*Lightly.*]

And you can't just let his dad take him to the park, 'cause, hey—"Where was Mom? Working?" He'll be in therapy the rest of his life—

[*Notices; matter of fact.*]

Harry? No, honey—put the little girl down. Put her down, babe.

[*Waits; easy.*]

Put her down and use your words, Harry.

[*Beat.*]

Not *those* words—

[*Laughs.*]

Hey, remind me to cancel Showtime—!

[*Smokes.*]

Well, at least the park beats . . . the playdate. The playdate is like the park—only in your house. The playdate, for a boy, is like, "I've already broken all my stuff, now I get to break yours." And then you have to learn a whole other language to communicate with the moms! Like last week I learned the word "ferberize"? Which means, if the kid cries *do not* pick him up. Just let him scream while you watch Bill Maher. And then, of course, you have to get involved with arts and crafts. I don't know, to me paper mache is like . . . vomit.

[*Sees—*]

Oh God, check this out. The little girl's got Harry's sippy cup and the mom is all like, "Don't touch that sippy cup! Dakota, put down the sippy cup! DROP THAT SIPPY CUP! He's probably not even vaccinated!"

[*Calls to son.*]

Harry, take your sippy cup and give back the Michele Obama Barbie.

[*Sighs.*]

Man, I love my kid . . . But sometimes I wish we'd met under different circumstances. Really, the only upside to all of this is . . .

[*Sees him; smiles.*]

Him.

[*Takes last drag.*]

So here's what they *don't* tell you in *What to Expect When You're Expecting*. Expect to give up smoking—eventually—because you can't bear to breathe secondary smoke on *him*. Expect to be unable not to open letters from UNICEF and Feed the Children and even Smile Train. Expect to cry in the Rite Aid parking lot when he's sick . . . and to bargain with a God you don't believe in to make him well. And expect to come back tomorrow with juice boxes and cookies—and fucking back 'em if you have to . . .

[*Rises; calls out.*]

Hey, Harry? Let's go get a doughnut, babe. And then we'll run through the fire hydrants. What? I don't know what that is, just wipe it on your shirt, couple of germs won't kill you.

[*To audience.*]

Later!

THE NORWEGIANS

C. Denby Swanson

Comic
BETTY, 20s–30s

BETTY, *a transplant from Kentucky, has lived in Minnesota for five long winters. Her heart has recently been broken by a Minnesota man of Norwegian descent. She could be speaking this as direct address to the audience, or she could be talking to another woman she's met in a bar.*

BETTY   The Norwegians. They are insidious. Dangerous. Clever. Strong. They are weatherproofed, as children, to not mind extreme cold or large flying bugs. Or Canada. They don't mind being close to Canada. They are insulated, somehow. Well trained for outdoor survival. Even babies. They kayak. Babies! Yes. They ski. It is like they are all little baby Navy SEALS. They learn to drive on frozen rivers, they learn how to slam on the brakes and spin wildly into the snow. Not babies. But teenagers. And on purpose—not like the rest of us, as an act of rebellion, or inadvertently because we don't know how to brake—but sanctioned, organized, they are trained to do it the right way. All their driver education classes take place outside in the winter on frozen rivers. All of them. On purpose. Training little Norwegian Jason Bournes. They are well fed, despite the limited window for agriculture, but they rarely get fat. In fact, they appear wholesome. And charming. And handsome. And perfect. And pure. But they're not. Don't be fooled. They prioritize social services, like elder care—they even call it *elder care*—and drug rehab for teenagers and independent living programs for the mentally ill—and they give to the arts with an unshakeable ferocity, even in difficult economic times, even in deficit years, as if they actually believe in those things, in the worth of those things, in the benefits of community. I asked one, I asked why, why these donations, why all this money going to artists and addicts and museums and public gardens? And he said, because otherwise it would be like living in Omaha, only further north. I swear, it's what he said directly to me. Asshole. . . . Think they're loyal, upstanding citizens? Think again. Norwegians started colonizing this country five centuries before Columbus. Greedy bastards. Never in large numbers. Secretly. Under the radar. Until they dominated the lumber trade and farming and fishing and crafts trades and back home there was a crisis and they decided to take over the flat, fertile land of our precious Midwest. Like they take over our flat, fertile women. There are five million of them now, in this country, committed to their homes and parks and neighborhood watch groups and to their extended families, too. "Family," right? You've seen *The Godfather*. But note this: In the last hundred years, almost no Norwegians have become Mormon. Okay? Right? You don't find that suspicious? Who can resist the Mormons these days? They knock on the doors of Jehovah's Witnesses and walk away with new converts. I mean, Mormons are freaking everywhere, and they have that pitch about saving the souls of your dead relatives, despite the fact that they're *dead*, if their souls are anywhere they're in Hell, you can imagine your great aunt suddenly yanked out of the fire—Oh, she says as the flames recede, I knew I could count on that one, my niece, she is such a nice person. But Norwegians, no. They're like, Well, now there's a hot dish, oh sure. I'm telling you, a practical people. Warm. Thoughtful. Destructive. Evil. Don't ever fall in love with one of them.

THE NORWEGIANS

C. Denby Swanson

Comic
BETTY, 20s–30s

At a bar at happy hour, BETTY *advises her new friend* OLIVE *about the challenge of boyfriend hunting in a place like Minnesota.*

BETTY   Here in Minnesota, you gotta find a lover before the first freeze or else it's just too late, you're iced in for a very long time, all alone. They don't tell you that when you move here, but it's true. You are iced in for all the short days, there are so many short days before the sun comes back and it begins to thaw. Short days and long nights. Long cold nights all alone, just the sound of the radiator in your apartment turning on, the knocking and the whispering of steam. Just leftover soup heated up midafternoon before the light fades. In fact, you make so much borscht that your poop turns red and you think it's blood and you have to have a tube with a camera on it shoved up your ass. On camera. In February. And the doctor aims the tube at you and says, "Here we go!" and then you watch your looming butt cheeks docked like the international space station by a tiny camera on a tube, like the space shuttle, right there on TV. It's that kind of cold, Olive. It's the cold of those bulky purple and yellow sweaters that you have to put on to take out the garbage, so that you're shapeless, like a big purple and yellow potato. That's you: a big plate of starch. You're just purple and yellow and shapeless and starchy, and you've just had a camera up your ass. . . . Unless of course you find a lover, and hold on to him, and you make your own steam, and knocking, and whispering, and you feed each other food from your hands, not soup but solid food, and you draw lines with ice cubes down each other's body, no one's cold then. No one's cold. No one's alone. So did you do that, Olive? Did you find someone before it froze? No. Oh, you tried, now, didn't you. But you failed. You didn't get a lover. No. No, you didn't. Because he left you. He froze you out. He left you to die. *That* is Minnesota nice, my new little friend. What I just did to you. That's what Minnesota nice feels like in your heart after five years. Five winters. That's all it takes. Unless of course you were raised here. Which I wasn't. I am from Kentucky.

THE NORWEGIANS

C. Denby Swanson

Comic
BETTY, 20s–30s

BETTY *and her new friend* OLIVE *are commiserating over their recent traumatic breakups.* OLIVE *believes in astrology but* BETTY *thinks it's a crock.*

BETTY   There's a reason the astrology column was always in the section of the newspaper with the comic strips and the weird little narratives about bridge games. Or the back of the magazine. Or the add-on to Facebook, like Farmville, or what, like what, like some stupid little app. But you take it seriously? Seriously? You take it seriously? You're one of those people? You, like, have an actual, like you have a person that you call? Jesus. Did your astrologer tell you that an awful man you loved was going to break your heart? Did she tell you, don't go to the fancy Italian restaurant that he Yelped and got all excited about, because it's a setup? Because you will be ambushed? Did she happen to mention that your boyfriend is a fucking power-hungry fucking asshole, by the way, clue number one is that he picked someplace special and expensive so that you won't scream and cry—he thinks you might, by the way, and he thinks he's being *nice* when he—when he pulls the plug and leaves you there to gasp for air and die. Weren't you wondering, sitting like a dumb ass, not breathing, not moving, as he says what he says, watching the truck come at you, bam! There's a forty-five dollar entrée and another glass of wine on its way, he says, graciously, "Get whatever you want, it's on me," and you don't wonder why you hadn't been warned by your FUCKING ASTROLOGER? Instead, you quietly sob with your head in your hands and people stare but you don't make a sound. Do you think your ex just had a better planet in his house that day than you?

THE NORWEGIANS

C. Denby Swanson

Comic
BETTY, 20s–30s

BETTY *has befriended* OLIVE *in a Minnesota bar at happy hour.
But neither of them is very happy.* OLIVE's *boyfriend recently
dumped her and* BETTY *is furious with the local Norwegians.*

BETTY   The Norwegians. And their Lutheran Church. Home
of orphan and refugee relocation services all over the
world. Their revered social services. Fuck me. Fuck them.
The Norwegians and their *gravlaks*. Does anyone even
know what that is? An alien word for, I don't know,
something fishlike. And fermented trout. Fermented.
Trout. And *lutefisk*—fish steeped in lye and then covered
in ashes. I mean, my god, fish, lye, and ashes. Fish, Lye &
Ashes. It sounds like a band name from the 1970s. Like,
a white R&B band. And their perpetually cheerful snow-
suits and their stupid local customs. They will stop in any
weather and help a stranger change their tire. I just want
to scream at them, I know you don't really mean that.
You cannot love people who make *gravlaks*. You cannot
love people who make *lutefisk*. You cannot FUCK people
who make elderberry wine, not an actual fuck, not a true
heartfelt beautiful intimate fuck, as I discovered. Late.
Or lingonberries. *Lingonberries*. If that doesn't bring up
dirty images in your head, I don't know what would. What
lover would let you serve them lingonberries? And my
god, hotdish: meat and Stovetop drenched in mushroom
soup and covered in Tater Tots. That's not even—that's
like casserole death. But Norwegians hand this "food" out
in the neighborhood when new people move in. When

there are potlucks. They think hotdish is welcoming. They think lingonberries are—Well. These are fearful, terrifying, terrible, very frightening things to serve people.

PARAFFIN (from The Hallway Trilogy)
Adam Rapp

Seriocomic
DENA, mid-30s

DENA *is talking to a friend about the many permutations that can occur in one's life-path.*

DENA   And so can bad things, but that's my point. We get so
stuck in our lives. I've been working at the same publishing
company for eight years. I walk the same route to work. I
take the elevator to the same floor, talk to the same agents
on the phone, attend the same boring editorial meetings. I
eat my lunch at roughly the same time every day. On
Saturdays I go to Film Forum or a play at Lincoln Center
and I have Sunday brunch with a sociable, articulate friend
whose outfit always equals his or her capacity to charm,
and then I usually come over here and spend a few hours
with Margo complaining about all of it and nothing really
changes. I mean, everyone here's probably been through
some cursory existential philosophy class. We've studied
our bit of Sartre and Kierkegaard and we've read William
Barrett and talked about action and inaction and what it
means to be alive and how most of us wind up middle-
aged zombies, etcetera, etcetera, but if you really stop to
think about it—if you really consider the possibility—isn't
it amazing how, on a candlelit night without the comfort
of cable television or the Internet or your porn collection,
or your favorite halogen lamp, whathaveyou, isn't it amazing how one rational choice could change your life? Let's
say I did go into Kevin's apartment and fuck his brains out.
Any number of things could happen. I could start shrieking
for you. I could get vertigo. I could freak out and curl into

a ball. I could have an Olympic orgasm. I could simultaneously get my period. I could get a fucking yeast infection and wind up spooning yogurt into my vagina! I could have multiple outerbody, extraterrestrial orgasms till my ears bled and not realize I've met my soul mate. We could fall in love. The possibilities are endless.

PUSSY
Laura Jacqmin

Dramatic
MARGOT, 20

MARGOT *is an American college student studying abroad. She is speaking to* ALISTAIR, *a very proper British M.A. student she met in a pub just a few hours earlier.* ALISTAIR *has been punched in the face by a stranger, and they have gone back to his flat to tend to his wound. Although* ALISTAIR *hopes to get lucky,* MARGOT *wants to get out of there, finding herself strangely attracted to the puncher back at the pub.*

MARGOT   I get all these e-mails from my friends, you know? Also doing study abroad? In Spain and Italy and France? "Met a dark, handsome man." "A dangerous man with a dicey past." And I believe them, because why wouldn't I? And the sex they have is epic. They need lube where they've never needed lube before. They miss class. They blow off trips to museums because they're so busy fucking in the broken-down, romantic, rust-stained flats of these dangerous men who smoke European cigarettes and have scarred knuckles, and the whites of their eyes are enormous and the pupils are dark pits. They fuck like they've never fucked before, and the fact that they're fucking strangers makes it better because it's crazy. It's crazy to sleep with an unknown person who radiates something—worrisome. It is violent and unwholesome and half terrifying. You're fucking someone who might murder you and it's fantastic and amazing and something to blog home about. In France and Italy and Spain. [*Beat.*] And I came to England. There is tea in England. And a certain breed of cow which is pleasing to the eye when it dots the hillsides. And the bottoms of the pint glasses say they're certified to hold a mathematically perfect pint by the Queen herself. I am not sure I was having the adventure I was meant to have.

QUASARS
Jennifer O'Grady

Dramatic
DANITA, early 20s

DANITA *is doing some sort of penance and has been assigned by a Catholic priest to help out* JOSH, *a sculptor, whose wife is dying of cancer.*

DANITA
[*To audience.*]

I never understood the expression "heavenly bodies." Because a) they're not bodies. And b) they're not in Heaven. Heaven is a place we can't see. Until we get there. If we get there. If it even exists. Planets aren't bodies, how could they be? They don't breathe. They don't sleep.

[*Casting a glance at* JOSH.]

They don't snore. [*Beat.*] They don't move in violent, unpredictable patterns. They're sitting ducks, just waiting for some meteor to strike and shatter them. But they're not bodies. Bodies have hands, and hands are for . . . Do you know what I keep seeing? I keep seeing his hands. I couldn't look at him, so I focused on the hands. And the nails, they were . . . They had red stuff underneath. Like dried blood. Not clay, it couldn't have been clay. Clay is for making things. Not tearing them down. [*Pause.*] I read there are things out in space called quasars. Nobody really knows what they are. I hadn't heard of them, so I looked it up, and it said: "An extremely remote celestial object, emitting exceptionally large amounts of energy." They look like stars. Scientists think they have black holes inside them, but that maybe they're the beginnings of new galaxies. Imagine, a whole new galaxy in the process of being born. There's hope in that, isn't there? I think that's hope.

RAT WIVES
Don Nigro

Seriocomic
JANET, 32

We are backstage at the Avenue Theatre in London, late on a blustery night in the autumn of 1896, just before a performance of Ibsen's Little Eyolf. *Four actresses are preparing to go on when* JANET ACHURCH—*tall, blond, and voluptuous, with a wayward actor husband,* CHARLES, *and a drinking problem—discovers that* MRS. PATRICK CAMPBELL *has been conspiring with the help of the other two actresses,* FLORENCE FARR *and* ELIZABETH ROBINS, *to take* JANET's *part away from her and move the show to the West End for a much more lucrative run without her.* JANET *is enraged and bitter and has started drinking again. This is the role of her life. She can't bear to give it up, and she's furious that the others have, in her eyes, betrayed her.*

JANET   It's theater that will kill me some day. Charles had the bright idea to take me on a grand theatrical tour of Australia, New Zealand, and Tasmania. All the great Tasmanian theaters. He thought there must be money in it somehow. It turns out they are not particularly big on Shakespeare in Tasmania. I was dreadfully ill, but we had to keep performing to pay our way home. They kept me going with alcohol and morphia until we got back to England, where the doctor informed me that my problem was an addiction to alcohol and morphia. Getting this role was such a great thing for me. And now you've stolen it from me. Stabbed me in the back. Stabbed me in the front. Stabbed me in my big, fat ass. The fact remains that I am doing the best work of my life here, in this wretched, dismal, wonderful clatfarting play, so of course you all feel compelled to conspire with a bunch of damned men to betray me so you can get rich dragging poor old Ibsen off kicking and screaming to the West End. We're doing a great thing here. We're doing Ibsen, difficult, boring, drab, cranky old Ibsen, and we're doing it as well as anybody has ever done it in the history of the world, and the first chance you three stupid whores get to cut my throat and take my part away and ruin it all, you jump at it, so goddamned anxious to make yourselves slaves once again to those greedy West End bastards with money in their pockets and shit between their ears. Aren't you the least bit ashamed of yourselves?

THE RELEASE OF A LIVE PERFORMANCE
Sherry Kramer

Seriocomic
NELL, late 20s–early 30s

A year ago, NELL *fell in love with a man with whom she had a one-night stand, and she doesn't know how to fall out of love with him. Everything—including other men—reminds her of him, so she has spent the past year remembering him in some very horizontal ways, with a different man every night. Her older sister,* COCO, *a married mother of two, has come back to Texas to rescue* NELL *from herself.* NELL *tries to tell* COCO *what it is like to be in the center of a world made out of longing.*

NELL Here's what I didn't tell you: There's no way back. There isn't anything I can do that doesn't make me think of him and when I think of him there's nothing left worth doing. Nothing. For a while I thought I had it licked. I took care of myself. I did things right. I felt the pleasure of doing things right. Things got very right for a while around here—the house was very clean and there was a lot of gourmet eating going on and I was to work on time and my bank balance was a piece of anal retentive art. Things got very right and I felt the pleasure of it, felt it fully, one day, for about thirty seconds. That was my mistake. My first, last, and always mistake. My always. I can make this chair—if I try very hard—I can make this ordinary chair *not* remind me of him. It's an act of the magic of hard work, but I'm not afraid of hard work. It can be done and I can do it. I can hard work systematically across this room like a minesweeper, disengaging every snap, crackle, and pop. But I can't break the hold in here. You walked into this house. You know—you must know—how warm and good it feels to have you walk into this house. And everything it feels like is him.

THE RELEASE OF A LIVE PERFORMANCE
Sherry Kramer

Seriocomic
NELL, late 20s–early 30s

A year ago, NELL *fell in love with a man she spent one night with, and she doesn't know how to fall out of love with him. Everything in the world—including other men—reminds her of him, so she's spent the year remembering him in some very horizontal ways, with a different man every night. Her older sister COCO, a married mother of two, has come to Texas to rescue NELL from her obsession. NELL tries to tell COCO what it's like to be in the center of a world made out of longing.*

NELL He's got a shirt. He's got all kinds of them. He puts them on. He takes them off. Sometimes I see shirts, and I want to see hundreds of 'em. I want to see them around me, in front of me, behind me, back through all recorded time. At times like that, I can't help myself. I jump in the car and drive to Neiman Marcus—the Men's Department. I run inside and I want to scream SHIRTS! ALL THESE SHIRTS COULD BE HIS SHIRTS! He could wear every shirt in the store. Oh Lord you should see me in Neiman Marcus. I've almost died there. Twice I've almost just pulled down a display on top of me and died. The fucking wonder of it all, Coco—that's what I'm talking about! It's the miracle of shirts! Like the famous shroud of Turin. I see him there. In every one of them. I walk into Neiman Marcus—and they can't tell. I look like a perfectly normal person—no one can tell! And boy do I love walking down the street, mingling with all those damn normal people—riding the same buses, sitting at the same luncheonettes, eating the same tasteless food. How I'd love it, someday at the luncheonette, some one day when everybody is eating the same runny mashed potatoes, the same dry turkey slice, how I'd love to stand up some one day and scream "You poor slobs! You poor, ordinary himless slobs! You're eating this shit but I'm thinking of him!" It's just one of those things. I just happen to love runny mashed potatoes and dry turkey slice. Always have.

THE RELEASE OF A LIVE PERFORMANCE
Sherry Kramer

Seriocomic
NELL, late 20s–early 30s

NELL *is talking to her sister* COCO, *who has come to Texas to save* NELL *from her obsession with a man with whom she had a one-night stand.* NELL *tells her what her obsession with him feels like.*

NELL   Imagine that you are lying on the fine, white sand on the shore of the Aegean Sea. It is a clear . . . warm . . . bright summer day. The Aegean's a sea you can see all in one place. It doesn't move around a lot like the big Seven do. And it's warm. All that land around it makes it warm. Imagine doing it with the Arctic Ocean—you're talking icebergs, you're talking chunks of dirty gray ice the size of Manhattan. The Aegean Sea is more green than blue, they say—I've never seen it. I suppose there are more things in a sea than there are in swimming pools—tuna and sharks and lots of microscopic swimming things—but I just can't picture doing it with a concrete, chlorinated pool. What would be the point? Are you relaxed now? That little talk was supposed to relax you. Get you primed. Imagine you are lying on your back on the fine, hard white sand on the shore of the Aegean Sea. You are looking up at the sky. It is more blue than any blue you have ever seen. You part your legs slightly. They open onto the bright, clear water. You hear the sound of the waves, breaking gently. You close your eyes. You draw in, with something inside you. It takes a moment or two, but gradually the water begins flowing up between your legs. The movement of the water feels—it feels—full. Whatever it is between your legs can suck, can pull, you suck and pull with. The water rushes in, past every soft, smooth place inside you. By now you know for sure where it is inside you that can suck and pull. By now you know how good it feels. By now you are ready to stop. Already tens of thousands of gallons have emptied into you. The level of the Aegean Sea, if you looked—but you don't look, you keep your eyes closed, you keep on sucking in—by now the level of the water is two, then five, then twenty feet lower, if you looked you'd see the great Aegean Sea shrinking, you'd see it funneling, disappearing into you, and you'd stop. But you don't stop. You'd see the slime and rock exposed banks, the naked bottom of the sea, the countless water creatures, gasping in the air, and you'd stop. You can't stop. You keep on, sucking in and in. And it feels wonderful, and it feels full and it will never fill you. Never.

SEED

Radha Blank

Comic
LATONYA: 25, African American

LATONYA *is the young, abrasive mother of* CHEE-CHEE, *a reluctant child genius from the Harlem projects. She stands behind the counter at her job at Duane Reade and takes the audience through a day in her life at work.*

LATONYA   E—ver-y where you go-oo . . . da da dada da da. Duane Reade Reade! Reade! Reade! Read the fucking signs to find your aisle/yes! I work here but I ain't gotta smile/no! I told you go to housewares/do I look like a pharmacist?!/that's a product for hair/no! I don't want your number/damn! ten minutes 'til break/a yo I didn't ring you up, so yo, that ain't my mistake/mis-ta ojo price check on register four!!!/uh-uh, sir fill that application out at the back of the store/miss you cain't return this! You ate the whole damn box/oooh! Rochelle who's that fine nigga in aisle two wit' the locks?/there's only one line!!!/damn, my feet straight hurt!!!/we got tic tacs, take your ass to Rite Aid if you want certs!/we a-bout to close! Bring all your purchases up!/girl, mista ojo got me down when I got night school—that's fucked up!/sir I ain't being rude/you got the fuckin' attitude!/oh no she didn't come to work wit' them old turn up shoes/who you tawkin' to Rochelle? I know you ain't tryna diss/hold up!/price check!/this is $3.49, you still want this miss?/price check!/this is $3.49, you still want this miss?/hold up!/price check!/this is $3.49, you still want this miss?/miss miss miss miss mis-fucking-understood!!!/people stare at Tonya like I ain't no good/but I ain't rude/ain't got no attitude/if ya stood in my Gucci boots/ya wouldn't call me rude' hold up!/price check!/this is $3.49, you still want this miss?/price check!/this is $3.49, you still want

this miss?/hold up!/price check!/this is $3.49, $3.49, $3.49/
ni-ni-ni-ni-ni-ni-ni-ni-nine/nine minutes 'til break/and I can
hardly wait/my son doing homework in the back/I need to
make sure he straight/just cause it's noisy here don't mean he
can't concentrate/rather that than wit them kids who hate/
ain't havin' it/I ain't lettin' him get flipped and kicked by kids
acting all jelly and shit/so quick/price check!/this is $3.49, you
still want this miss?/price check!/this is $3.49, you still want
this miss?/hold up/price check!/this is $3.49, you still want
this miss?/price check!/this is $3.49, you still want this miss?
Hold up!

[*Sees son.*]

CHEE-CHEE?!?!

SEVEN INTERVIEWS
Mark Dunn

Dramatic
DEANNE, late 20s

DEANNE SPRAWLEY, *a recent widow, and her father,* HUCK
GLEASON, *are summoned to the office of* MS. HENDERSON *to
discuss* DEANNE'*s son* TOMMY'*s behavior in school following the
death of his father (and DEANNE's husband).* DEANNE *learns that*
TOMMY'*s behavior at this conservative Christian private school
has warranted his suspension from the school.* DEANNE *comes to
see that* TOMMY'*s struggles with his religious faith (he now questions the existence of God), which mirror her own, have placed
into strong perspective the very definition of religious faith. Are we
never to question that which is put in front of us by church elders,
or should Christians exercise their God-given brains and tap into
their innate capacity for compassion, even when it might be messy
and break certain sacrosanct rules? Here,* DEANNE *puts all of this
into the context of her own life and tragic circumstances.*

DEANNE   I used to believe in a lot of things. I have lost my
husband, Ms. Henderson. My own faith has been severely
tested. Perhaps I've lost that too. Tommy and I—with my
father's help—we're just trying to get through each day as
it comes. It really sucks, Ms. Henderson. Life sucks. God isn't
smiling on Tommy and me right now. I don't blame Tommy
for anything he says or does. If he's hurting another child,
that's another matter. But questioning the existence of God
when circumstances don't give you much of a reason to
believe—I don't think that's such an odd thing to be doing.
It tells me that Tommy is working his way through this the
best he can. And I understand the anger. And I understand
the betrayal because I feel it too. But what I *don't* under-

stand is people like *you*, Ms. Henderson. Controlling kinds of people. That's what this school is—I've come to see it now. You control little minds. You put little minds in very tight boxes and punish those who don't stay put. Faith to me has always been a journey of discovery—an exploration. I have never taken anything at face value. My husband taught me to question. We had late night theological arguments. I'm not a stupid woman, Ms. Henderson. But even stupid people still have brains enough to think for themselves and pride enough not to be spoon-fed one particular way of looking at the world.

SEVEN INTERVIEWS
Mark Dunn

Dramatic
JULIANA, 30s

JULIANNA BUCHNER, *mother of a young daughter who has been brutally raped by a man whom the criminal justice system has allowed to walk free, has decided to take matters into her own hands by hiring a hit man to kill her daughter's assailant. When asked by the contract killer in the interview in which the contract is made to murder the rapist if she will be able to live with herself after he makes the hit, she answers through this monologue—a demonstration of how deeply her revenge obsession has taken hold. At the same time, the monologue expresses JULIANNA's fervent wish that "none of this should ever have happened." She is tortured, she is painfully regretful, but the overriding emotion is pure hatred, fueled by sudden, fortuitous empowerment. Circumstances have transformed her into a criminal too, and she seems almost exultant over this outcome.*

JULIANNA   It's all I've thought about since he walked out of that courtroom. I wake up in the middle of the night wanting him dead. I stand in the produce section of Kroger's wanting him dead. I sit at green traffic lights with people blaring their horns and I want him dead. I've never wanted anything so much in my life. Except . . . to be dead myself. But I have to stay alive. I have to nurse Kimmie back to health. I have to be her mommy. There is one other thing. One other thing, Mr. Gampion, that I wish for more. It's an impossible wish: that this should never have happened. That I should have Kimmie back the way it was before. I wish to turn back the clock, Mr. Gampion. But I can't. And I can't go out some night and drive my car off an overpass.

So I do the only thing I *can* do: I ask you to end the life of the man who tried to end my daughter's life, and who ended up destroying it nonetheless. That is what I can do. I don't care what God thinks. I don't care what the Bible says. I don't care what compassion requires. I care nothing about any of those things. Kill him, Mr. Gampion. Do it slow or do it quick. Do it however you see fit. And know that I will never change my mind. It won't put Kimmie back the way she was. It won't put Bill and me back the way we were. But I want it done. Now *I* get to be the criminal. Now it's *my* turn. Good-bye, Mr. Gampion.

SEX CURVE
Merridith Allen

Comic
ROBYN, 27–32

ROBYN, *a sex-lit writer and columnist, decides she needs to edu-cate her two roommates about how to pick a potential boyfriend.*

ROBYN   "The compatibility trifecta." There are three key fac-tors which will help determine how a man will act. The first factor is porn. Yes, it may be uncomfortable for you, the po-tential love interest, to immediately dive into your potential mate's porn collection. However, his sexual habits, stamina, and personality are all reflected through his porn.

[*She looks over to LUCAS, who is chewing. She swats at him.*]

Lucas, are you chewing gum? Spit it out. Anyway, the second factor is friends. Get to know his friends, and you get to know the side of himself that you may not see or know or come across otherwise. Friends have all the right character-revealing stories. Lastly, look at his habits. This is an extension of factor one, but includes both sexual and nonsexual habits. Things such as masturbation frequency, diet, exercise, sleep cycle, work schedule, hobbies, and past relationship patterns all fit into this category. After a thor-ough investigation, if the result is pleasing, then go ahead, hop into bed with the guy.

THE SINS OF REBETHANY CHASTAIN

Daniel Guyton

Comic
REBETHANY, early 20s

REBETHANY *is a sweet and syrupy Southern belle, who has just been arrested for murder. She is talking to a TV reporter. Eventually, she does get around to telling the reporter why she did it, after telling them this story.*

REBETHANY   Hi. My name's Rebethany. Rebethany Anne Chastain. I know, it sounds British, don't it? Yeah, my momma was from England. No, not the country. You know, New Hampshire? [*Pause.*] God, that's a long ways away. My daddy was Alabaman, born and raised. Except then he moved to Arkansas when he was two, so I guess he wasn't really raised here actually. Although . . . Well . . . Does that count as being raised here if you were two? I don't know. Anyway, they were good people, maw and paw. Very good people. [*Pause.*] Until the drought came. Summer a '97. I'll never forget it. Paw came in one day saying, "Who let the dang hose run dry?!?" Of course, I had done it. I was cleanin' off my bicycle, on account'a it was dusty. You see, we live in a dirt road, all a' way up in Elmer, nearest to Kentucky? And I was really proud of my bicycle. I was the only girl in Elmer with a bicycle! At least one with wheels on it. Of course Maybelline Ohmer had a bicycle also, but it was just a frame. She found it at the old churchyard, underneath a pile of leaves. The bishop said she could have it if she'd finish cleanin' up the leaves. Of course she did it. Maybelline Ohmer had to have everything. We were all so jealous. It didn't even have a seat or nothing. It was just a frame. But lord, she'd sit on that thing for hours. No wonder she got tetanus in her leg that summer? And she lost control of her vagina. I swear, the entire cooch just fell right off of her! Least that's what her boyfriend Russell told me. And he should know, cuz he was her brother. Anyway, daddy came home one day, and he'd made a bundle, playing poker? And he came up to our double-wide with a brand-new shiny bicycle for me. With a seat and everything! So I used to ride that bike past Maybelline Ohmer's house every morning before school. And I'd say, "Hey Maybelline! How's that frame of yours doing?" And she would call me dirty names. I mean, really un-Christian-like things, you know? Until one day Maybelline stopped coming out. I thought, "Surely her momma must be spankin' her for all them nasty things she said." But no, come to find out, it was just her vagina fallin' off.

[*She folds her arms.*]

I guess that was just God's way of punishing her for all them nasty things she said.

SKIN & BONE

Jacqueline Goldfinger

Comic
EMMA, mid-20s

EMMA *has arrived at the home of two old ladies,* MIDGE *and* MADGE, *who operated a bed-and-breakfast there years ago, where* EMMA's *late mother once stayed. She has been rearranging the stuff in the house so it looks like it did in the old brochure she found in her mother's things.*

EMMA   Why wouldn't you know better what's right in your own home than some stupid little girl? Some little pea brain who don't know her own strength and accidentally breaks a zirconium-studded Princess Diana glassware set that her foster brother was gonna sell on eBay to pay for the removal of his "I Heart Mom" tattoo because Mom's turned into a real grumpy old bitch, and then her boyfriend dumps her because she accidentally fed his pet rats to his pet snake when he's on a men's retreat in the New Orleans French Quarter with a real sweet girl from his Bible study class named Suzy Sucker, and then who goes to work and gets mixed up when people shout at her through the microphone at the McDonald's drive-thru so she pushes all the wrong buttons on the register when there's a long five o'clock line and backs traffic up all the way to Route 6 so she gets sent to work the milkshake swirl machine but the milkshake swirl machine won't freeze right no more and her boss says it's her fault so they're gonna take repairs out of her paycheck so then she's sent to work the French fry fryer but then the grease in the French fry fryer catches fire so she tries to put it out with a bucket of water and when she pours the water on the French fry fryer, the French fry fryer explodes and catches the burger maker on fire and then the burger maker catches the fish-o-fillet press on fire and then the fish-o-fillet press catches the bun toaster on fire and the bun toaster catches the entire McDonald's on fire and it goes up in a big whoosh and the assistant manager's pissed and he's also her landlord so she loses her job and gets kicked from her apartment and so she takes her last fifteen dollars and heads out to the only place she knows to go, the last place her momma was, so maybe she'll find something good there. Something good in the last place that anything good ever happened before everything went bad and maybe she can start all over again, Miss Madge. Start something different and keep it good.

A SNOWFALL IN BERLIN
Don Nigro

Dramatic
ROSA: 25, Mexican

ROSA *is a young Mexican actress, who spends the play in the
bathtub in which she was found drowned and possibly murdered.
She was starving in New York when taken in by* NATASHA, *a bril-
liant but troubled director of independent films, and thrust into a
central role, that of a girl who drowns in a bathtub. As* DETECTIVE
MULLIGAN *tries to understand what happened to her, we hear her
speak and see fragments of her life. In this play death is seen as
a kind of dream state in which* ROSA *can communicate with the
other characters as they remember her.*

ROSA   I came to New York to study acting. I grew up in foster
   homes. I had nobody. I wanted a fresh start. I had so many
   hopes when I got here. But I hated acting school. Acting
   is this. No, acting is that. This system. No, that system. This
   teacher is God. No, this teacher is God, that teacher is the
   Devil. Worship me. No, worship me. They smile and cut your
   throat. It all seemed so unhealthy to me. I thought if I just
   got out there and started working, everything would be all
   right. So I dropped out and began auditioning. But there
   were so many things they wouldn't even consider me for
   because of my accent. And my hair. In American culture,
   there is no such thing as a blond Hispanic girl. So I couldn't
   get roles because I had a Spanish accent, and I couldn't get
   Hispanic roles because my hair was the wrong color. So I
   dyed my hair, but then I was just a girl with dyed hair and
   an accent. I was running out of money. I wasn't eating. I was
   just at the edge of the abyss, looking down into the water.
   I went to a diner, late at night, and ordered some soup. I

didn't have enough to pay, but my friend Megan worked there, and usually she'd find a way to get me something to eat. But Megan was off that night, and when the manager realized I didn't have any money, he said he was going to call the police. And I started to cry. And a couple of tables over, there was this beautiful Russian woman, arguing with an Italian woman about something. And she looked over and saw me crying, and how the manager was treating me, and Natasha just jumped right out of her seat, like a lioness defending her cub. She scared the hell out of the manager, bought me dinner, and listened to my story. She was so kind to me. And she said to Emilia, right then and there, "This is her. This is the girl in the tub. I had no idea what she was talking about, and it crossed my mind for a second or two that I'd fallen into the hands of a dangerous lunatic, but I didn't care. She was so wonderful. And they took me in. And gave me a place to stay. And the next day we were shooting the movie. It was all like a dream. Natasha is like a dream.

SOMEBODY/NOBODY

Jane Martin

Comic
LOLI, 20s

LOLI *has managed to escape small-town life in Flatt, Kansas,
where she was a truck mechanic. Into her tiny apartment in Los
Angeles bursts a movie star named* SHEENA, *covered in blood,
seeking sanctuary.* SHEENA *hires* LOLI *to be her Personal Assistant
and has renamed her* PRISCILLA, *since that's a requirement for the
job, and sent her off to tell* SHEENA*'s agent,* GALAXY, *that* SHEENA
has gone to Abu Dhabi. "PRISCILLA" *has just returned and tells*
SHEENA *what happened.*

LOLI   Okay suite one thousand. Now, I went in where you wait
. . . kinda stood on the edge of it 'cause I didn't want to put
my dirty shoes on that Chinese rug. But finally I just yelled
out, "Sheena Keener's gone to Abu Dhabi!" and boy, all hell
brook loose . . . this alarm bell went off, people whanged
out of doors, and these vituperous dachshunds got loose,
went after the reception lady. Boy, she vaulted over her
counter thing but she knocked over this espresso setup
which spilled on this dandy man's white linen suit and he
lets out this yell and his chair tipped over backwards so his
cigar set these skinny curtains on fire which set off some
sprinkler things and then bam! This young girl with those
murderous eyes comes out this golden door, and all these
wet people backed up against the wall . . . shoot, even the
dachshunds backed up and she walked up real, real close
to me and says, kinda sweet and poisonous, did I know who
Louis the Fourteenth was? And I did, I studied that. And she
said she was the Louis the Fourteenth of Hollywood, her
name being Galaxy-bigger-than-a-star, So I went into Abu

Dhabi real strong and she asked who it was I figured I was?
So I said I was Priscilla the Seventh, your personal assistant
and she said . . . giving me the death eye . . . that if you had
run off she would flay me alive, and she claps her hands
and this dachshund launches at me but I duck and it lands
on her, and while the two of them go at it like the lions and
the Christians, I ran down seventeen flights of stairs and
got me a cab ride back and here I am. Oh, stopped off on
the way home and got you a mango.

SOUL SAMURAI

Qui Nguyen

Dramatic
LADY SNOWFLAKE, 20s

LADY SNOWFLAKE *is a samurai vampire, confronting her former lover,* DEWDROP, *who she believes left her to die in the streets five years earlier.* DEWDROP *has just killed* LADY SNOWFLAKE*'s boss, and they are facing off on the Brooklyn Bridge at dawn.*

LADY SNOWFLAKE   Oh, I'm not am I? I'm not the first girl you ever loved? The first girl whose name you scribbled in your notebook with hearts all around it? I'm not the first girl you ever let take you to heaven and back with just the use of a tongue and forefinger? What? Too graphic for you? OK, how's this for PG-13? Am I not the first girl you left dying in the streets five years ago because your chicken-shit ass wasn't brave enough to open the goddamn car door to let me in? "Open the door. Open the fucking door." That meant for you to let me in, not for you to drive away, ya dumb cunt. And secondly. Oh yes, bitch, there's a secondly. Secondly, to follow up your utter failure at being my greatest love, it took you over a half decade to finally come back to get me some revenge. Shit, bitch, I got cans of Spam that rot faster than that. And Spam, as you might know since you're a fucking Filipino and all, takes a goddam long time to fucking rot. You abandoned me, Dew. And the truth is, I'm glad I'm what I am now. And now because of the superpowers or the amazing kinkilicious hot outfits. I'm glad, 'cause if I weren't, that shit you done to me woulda hurt pretty fucking bad. So, see, there's a boon to not having a soul, little Samurai. It makes living live a lot easier. Ain't that something? But worry not. I'm not mad at ya. No way. You gave me a gift tonight after all. I'm the new Kingsborough King. And it's all because of you. Let me look at you, baby. I'm glad to be able to see that gorgeous face of yours again. That face I once loved. A face that once loved me. You and I were meant to be queens, baby girl. We were meant to ride the world, not stand here on this old bridge fighting like a pair of some sad samurai. Let me give you what you deserve. Oh, it's me. Every fine fiber, every delectable inch. I'm that girl you loved and lost and now see again. And I'm asking you—girl who once broke my heart—are you really going to kill me?

SOUSEPAW
Jonathan A. Goldberg

Dramatic
REPTILE GIRL, late teens

REPTILE GIRL *is a carnie performer.* RUBE WADDELL, *once a great baseball pitcher but now a has-been who dreams of making it back to the game, has enticed her to his seedy hotel room for a private performance. Here, she talks about her life at the carnival.*

REPTILE GIRL   I lost count of my age. Hadn't mattered. When you got no standard schedule—don't really matter how many years gone by. The only real time I counted was when I was pregnant and even then it was only so I could give it up. But I am young and I am beautiful. And my scars are beautiful and my breasts and elbows and all of me. This one fella from New York comes to do the taxes for the circus. He stays for a while. Don't know his name they just call him Yankee or The Jew. His breath was always sour and he was always with a cigarette in his lips. His hair was gone from where he'd wiped his head with frustration. Like this.

[*Demonstrates.*]

He was all work. But one night we were somewhere near St. Louis by the river. It was hot and I went down to this place to swim. I swim naked. 'Cause . . . 'cause I feel like a salamander. I like to spread my fingers wide when I swim—feel the water slip through them like I'm letting something escape. I look up and see a glint on the shore. It's the Jew the light was off his glasses. He was just watching me. I swam over and got out of the water. I don't know why, maybe I wanted him to see me or I just wanted to get out or. And I sit next to him on the bank. My body on the grass. He asks me: "Aren't you embarrassed?" I didn't know what he was saying? He says something about how people invented clothes because of shame. Because being naked scares us. I asked him if I scared him. He said yes. I asked him why. And he just looked out and the night bugs kept on kicking up a racket and he picked up a stone and chucked into the water. He said how many girls must have passed through their youth never being naked and how much that must have hurt them. That in their old age how they must have wished to be sixteen again and run naked. Because back then they were all beautiful, even the ugly ones were never more beautiful than when they were young. And I asked him again why I scared him. He took out a cigarette and lit it.

STICK FLY
Lydia R. Diamond

Dramatic
CHERYL: late teens, African American

CHERYL *is spending her summer working as a housekeeper for a wealthy black family that owns a home on Martha's Vineyard. Here, near the end of the play, she confronts the family and, in particular, the father, about the truth of who he really is.*

CHERYL   I know Dr. LeVay. I know everything. And how the hell didn't not one of you sorry mothafuckas not figure it out . . . because you don't think 'bout nothin' but yourselves and your damn socioeconomic bantering, and bugs, and relationship dysfunction and shit. Seriously, the most self-involved bullshit people. [*Beat.*] Mrs. LeVay found out. She came home and told that man that she knew he was my daddy. Then she kicked your ass out the house, didn't she Dr. LeVay. And he brings his sorry ass up here. So you knew and you looked me in the face and said, you know, how I like my sandwiches, or some shit like that . . . That's right. DAD! O.K. O.K. [*Long pause.*] So, two weeks ago . . . One of Mrs. LeVay's friends invites her to sit on the board at the high school where I'm supposed to be on scholarship, right. It's a big ole' lunch in some sort of fancy oak-paneled room . . . . This is how it got told to my mama anyway, you know there's a network of maids . . . they talk . . . So, The Ladies who Lunch are lunching, and this woman says, Michelle, it's so generous what your husband has been doing for that girl all these years. Eighteen years . . . you can keep your mouth shut for five more minutes. . . . Imagine it . . . you could smell the money, all those skinny rich bitches staring at her over their shrimp salads. Four years now, right,

Michelle? Mrs. LeVay's been set up. Your daddy's been paying my tuition there since I started. Fought to have me accepted, but insisted it remain on the DL. [*To* KIMBER.] That's "down low." Twenty-five thousand a year. So, this is the thing that's the craziest. It wasn't that Mrs. LeVay was broken up about a kid who shares her own kids' gene pool washing her crusty sheets, no, the tragedy was that it got out. She calls my mother, threatens to fire her . . . calls her all out of her name, after Ma's been so quiet about it all these years . . . and threatens to take us to court for libel. I'm supposed to have a daddy got shot in the Gulf . . . And you knew . . . how can you live with yourself?

SUNSET BABY
Dominique Morisseau

Dramatic
NINA: late 20s, African American

NINA, *a hustler and drug dealer, has been confronted by her father, a former radical political activist who has done a long stretch in prison, and whom she grew up never knowing. He's just gotten out and wants to reconnect with her, and wants some letters she may have that were written to him by her mother, also a radical activist, who descended into drug addiction and, eventually death.* NINA *bitterly resents her father and all he stands for.*

NINA   I don't give a fuck about your fight. Fuck your progress! This is your progress, nigga. Me. Here! I'm your fuckin' progress. This is what you achieved. Shit. Deal with that, nigga. Deal with the sacrificial fuckin' lamb to your better world. And what is better, hunh? What the fuck did you achieve? My mama died with a broken heart waitin' on your progress. You were the muhfucka who wouldn't throw her a damn bone. You want these letters so bad? Why'd you never write her? I'm not talking about them scrap pages of your ideas and meditations while you were locked up and gettin' your brain swollen with information on politics and philosphies and whatever. I'm not talking about your intellectual masturbation on a fuckin' piece of prison paper. I'm talking reciprocity. I'm talking speaking from the core of your gotdamn heart instead soundin' like a fuckin' activist robot. I know her better than you ever will. I listened to her pine over your worthless ass. Listened to her talk about what she thought made you such a gotdamn hero. How you stood up for niggas gettin' railroaded by the justice system, how you stood up for anybody being brutalized by the cops, how you protested corporations helping to fund apartheid, how you did all this shit for the whole gotdamn free world. But when she told you she loved you, what you do hunh? When she told you she wanted you to settle the fuck down and be with her, what you do, hunh? You stand up for that shit?

TEN CHIMNEYS
Jeffrey Hatcher

Dramatic
UTA, late 20s

UTA HAGEN *has returned to Ten Chimneys, the Wisconsin estate of* ALFRED LUNT *and* LYNN FONTANNE, *where a few years previously she rehearsed the Lunts' production of* The Seagull, *in which she played* NINA. *She has been estranged from the Lunts ever since. Here, she is talking to a man who manages the estate.*

UTA   Do you remember driving me to Milwaukee late one night so I could catch a train? My mother died that night. By the time I got there, the doctors said I couldn't go into her room, that if she saw me she'd realize how serious her condition was—so I never saw her alive again. After the funeral, I went back to New York and we started rehearsals. Everyone was very kind, Mr. Lunt and Miss Fontanne were very kind.

[*Beat.*]

We were doing *The Sea Gull*. On Broadway. I'd gotten good notices, and my agent called me to say I had an offer to be in a new show when *The Sea Gull* closed. It was a comedy, for Broadway, the part was perfect for me. All that had to happen was that the Lunts release me from going on the tour. But they said no. "It's the height of unprofessionalism to leave one show for another." I'd signed a contract to go on the road for nine months just like the rest of the cast. So I did.

[*Beat.*]

We were doing *The Sea Gull*. We were in Philadelphia. It was a Sunday night, after a four-show weekend, very hot.

I was in my room at the hotel. I was exhausted, I hadn't slept for days—so I took a pill, just one so I could sleep through the night. At the hospital the doctor said I'd swallowed a dozen. Miss Fontanne and Mr. Lunt were so concerned they sent me to a psychiatrist. He told them I wasn't in any condition to continue the tour and should be released from my contract. They said no. "The stage is the best medicine." So I stayed.

[*Beat.*]

We were doing *The Seagull*. Chicago. I was standing in the wings, waiting for my cue. In the last act Nina is supposed to have gone mad. All during rehearsals, I couldn't understand how a simple, happy young girl could suddenly go mad. And then I remembered something Sydney said in this room about his wife. He said she'd never been well, he just hadn't noticed. I realized Nina didn't *suddenly* go mad. She'd *always* been this troubled, erratic, unstable personality, but all the men misread the symptoms of distress as signs of passion and fire. In a flash, I knew how to do the role, start to finish. And then I noticed how quiet it was on stage. I looked and there was Mr. Lunt. He'd just said my entrance cue. If I went on, the audience would never notice. And then I thought how they wouldn't let me go, and I couldn't quit. So I stood there. Mr. Lunt said his line again. I didn't move. Then he said it a third time. And then I went on. The next morning I left the company. They didn't try to stop me this time. They moved on to the next town. They were doing *The Seagull*.

THALASSA
Scott Sickles

Dramatic
JANINE, early to mid-20s

JANINE *was to have been married today, but her fiancé drowned in the Mediterranean just days before. Despairing, her plan to follow him into the sea and join him has hit a snag: she's pregnant. Uncertain as to how to proceed, she encounters a stranger (DEREK, who lost his own significant other a year ago and had the same idea) and enlists his help in trying to figure things out.*

JANINE He asked me to go with him. Just on the boat. Jerry said it would be a great way for me to overcome my fear of the water. And I promised I would do it. I went to the pier, put on my life vest . . . I even got in. Then the boat rocked and I got right back out. Lucky me.

[*Beat.*]

The only reason I'm still alive, that I'm still here is that I broke a promise to the one person I swore I would never break a promise to. And now he's dead . . . and I'm a ghost. I'm supposed to be down there with him and if I'm supposed to be there, then . . . And all I am asking for . . . all I want is one measly sign, some indication . . . I'm not looking for a sign from God! I'm looking for a sign from . . .

[*Beat.*]

Look, all I want to do is stand there, and . . . and I'll wait for him to tell me what to do . . . if he wants me to stay out here and do this all by myself, which I don't think I can . . . Or if he wants us . . . That way, we can all be together. But either way, I just want one day . . . this day . . . to feel like he has his arms around me, holding me, telling me that one way or the other everything's going to be all right.

THIS IS FICTION
Megan Hart

Dramatic
CELIA, mid-30s

CELIA *is speaking to her younger sister,* AMY. AMY *has just come home to tell* CELIA *that she's written a book about their mother, a troubled alcoholic who died in a car accident years earlier.* CELIA *was her mother's de facto caretaker in her later years while Amy was living in the city pursuing her artistic dreams. She is vehemently against* AMY *publishing the book, as she feels* AMY *cannot tell this story, having not been there in her mother's final days, nor on her final night.*

CELIA   You want to know why mom drove herself home that night? I was taking a drawing class. I didn't tell anyone. I just had the crazy thought that maybe I could go back to school—focus more on my art. That night was bad—I almost didn't go—I was fucking dreading class. We were working on figure drawing with charcoal, and I was terrible at it. It was all big hands and tiny heads. My people looked like victims of that drug pregnant women were taking back in the seventies. Awful. But I had this incredible teacher—Sam—I never had a teacher who told us to call him by his first name before. And Sam kept telling me it would happen if I kept working. And that I had a gift even if I couldn't see it yet. So that night I made myself go. I picked up a piece of charcoal and I went to work on my tiny heads. And I started to cry a little bit, if you can believe it. Just to myself. Sam saw I was having a meltdown and he came over. He took the charcoal out of my hand and handed me a pallet with three blobs of red, yellow, and blue paint. He told me to take a good look at the model, his thigh muscles, the way his stomach moved. And then he turned my easel around so my back was to the model I was supposed to be drawing. I was like, "What the hell am I supposed to do now?" And he said, "Don't look back. Just paint." I started with one red splotch. Then I did another. Then it just took over. It was like I was above myself looking down at my hands moving across the page in these big stripes of color. I painted the entire easel, the mat the paper was clipped to. I would have moved to the walls if Sam hadn't stopped me. He looked at what I had done and he said, "Well there you are. I was wondering when we'd find you."

[CELIA *is a little bit choked up though she'd never admit it.*]

When I looked around, everyone was starting to pack up. Class was over. But I wasn't finished. I was vibrating, I was hovering above the floor. Sam said, "Stay. If you want. The door will lock behind you." So I stayed. [*Beat.*] When I got to the bar, her usual stool was empty. I think you know the rest. A fucking drawing class.

[*Beat.*]

I've rewritten a million versions in my head. What if I hadn't stayed. What if I showed up? What if mom made it home? What if you stayed here? What if I left? What if, what if. You wrote this book—I could write a hundred of them.

TOURISTS OF THE MINEFIELD
Glenn Alterman

Dramatic
ILSA, 30s

ILSA *sits alone at the nearly empty bar. After a moment she turns towards the audience, speaks softly.*

ILSA I always know them; well, I can usually spot them, right away. It's like a sixth sense or something. They're usually the ones talking too loud, making with the jokes, laughing too loud. Talking; talking to . . . whoever's around, next to them, next bar stool. Maybe their friends, maybe not. Maybe they're people they just met, I don't know, doesn't matter. So I sit, and wait, and watch. I want to be sure. I like bars that are bars, not clubs or lounges. Just good old-fashioned *drink bars* where people can sit and talk and hear. And the lighting's usually dim, and the music's not too loud. So soon I'll have a drink or two to loosen up. As I continue to watch them. I need to be certain. By now I know all the signs. . . . As the night goes on, they get louder and their laughter . . . It's usually around then that I mosey over, get closer, a bar stool nearby. Let them see me, know I'm there. By now they're up on their drinks and are very accepting of all new friends. And so I ingratiate myself, let them know I think they're funny, as I laugh at their unfunny jokes. As the drinks keep coming. And soon, well sooner rather than later, the two of us become engaged in some frivolous conversation about . . . doesn't matter. So I suggest that we move away from the bar, somewhere quieter. "Sure," they'll say. And we do. Perhaps to a darkened corner somewhere, or maybe a small out-of-the-way table. And soon, somewhere in that shadow, I look into their eyes and ask [*Very softly, caring.*], "So . . .

what's going on?" Perhaps it's how I say it; like I mean it, like I really want to know. Because usually at that moment, their expression changes, they look at me as if . . . as if for the very first time. I mean here we've been talking . . . And so I say it again, "What's going on? Tell me." Then there is that moment where the tide changes, where the curtain opens. Where everything is different than it was just a moment before. And then they talk, begin *really* talking; but now their voice is much softer.

[*A beat.*]

Sometimes . . . sometimes it's about grief. Sometimes, it's about the end of a long love affair or a marriage that ended. Or sometimes it's about something that happened a long time ago—something that still haunts them. But it always seems to be about loss. Pain. And then they talk, and talk, and talk. But they usually speak very softly. And then they cry; almost always. And sometimes I cry with them. Maybe even hold their hand. Finally . . . I feel. Finally I feel what . . . !

[*A beat.*]

And sometimes they make these small childlike sounds. Not words, but sounds. And I sit there, and listen, and let them know I'm there. Because in that moment, I care—very much. We are not strangers anymore. And we both sit there until, well, there's nothing more to say, so we're silent for a while. There's just bar noise and music. And perhaps someone else laughing too loud at the bar. And I know it's time for me to go. And I do; without much fanfare. Sometimes I tell them my name, my first name. And sometimes I don't. I just leave, smile, say good night, wish them the best. And then I go . . . home.

THE TUTOR
Kate Mulley

Comic
MEREDITH, late 20s

MEREDITH, *a Yale Law School graduate turned SAT tutor, is record-*
ing a video diary entry for her used-underwear website.

MEREDITH   I know what you're thinking: How does a nice
   smart girl get involved in petty sex trade? Two parts neces-
   sity, one part childhood repression. But seriously: I read
   an article about it. It's 3L spring and despite having some
   pretty impressive credentials and a desire to change the
   world, I can't find a job. My father, who's a *philosopher*, tells
   me I should think outside the box for once and focus on the
   present rather than the future. So I spend a lot of time pe-
   rusing the Internet in hopes that it would pique my imagi-
   nation. One week I decided I would join the Peace Corps,
   until I realized that I didn't really want to live in any of the
   countries they go to. After that I thought I would open up
   a cupcake store, but student loans and a lack of decorating skills made that plan pretty ludicrous. Not to mention
   it's an utter cliché at this point. And then I read an article
   about used-underwear retail. And the more research I did,
   the more intrigued I was. When you feel like you were the
   least sexually active girl at a school like Brown, sometimes
   you need to prove your past wrong by living in the present.
   So, I enlisted a photographer friend to help me with pictures, used my nerdy high school computer skills to build a
   kickass site, and went live a month later. It started out slow,
   but an ingenious viral campaign and some innuendo-laden
   tweeting made my site the one to watch pretty quickly.
   By the time graduation rolled around I was making bank

and was too busy to study for the bar, which I determined was unnecessary anyway. That fall, I started SAT tutoring to give myself a slightly more legitimate supplement to my sexy online business. And voila. A year later, I'm financially solvent, in constant contact with seventy-five perverted men and five women, and the lingerie store down the street calls me when any new items come in stock. And you wonder why I haven't had sex in a month?

UNDISCOVERED PLACES
D. Richard Tucker

Dramatic
JULIE, 28

JULIE has met her father, DAN, *previously unknown to her, for the first time. Alone with* DAN's *wife,* JULIE *expresses her feelings and her confusion on how to handle the situation.*

JULIE   Sometimes, he'll say something and I'll note the inflection in his voice, or a gesture, or a mannerism, and I think, "That's me. This guy is mimicking me," and then I realize—I got that from him. It's kind of weird. I guess I had an inkling that there might be more to it . . . than what I knew. His name isn't on my birth certificate, so, well, it made me question my mom's story. She didn't talk about it. She just said it was in the past and we needed to move forward. I guess a big part of me just moved on. I thought about looking for more info on him, but I didn't have much to go on. I'm still trying to get past the whole, "Why did you hide my daddy?" thing. I don't know how I would have dealt with that . . .
if I had been in her shoes. Of course, it's easy to say what should have happened, but if there's anything that the Army taught me, it's that you never can be sure how you'll respond until you come face to face with the problem. I knew a girl in high school who was adopted, and when she was sixteen, she went through this huge effort to find her birth parents. It seemed crazy to me for her to spend time and money trying to find people who chose not to be in her life. My roommate in college was really close to her family, even though they were constantly making her mad. Her mom did all kinds of passive aggressive stuff and her dad didn't pay her much attention, and she would

constantly complain about how awful they were . . . and yet, she would call them almost every day and spend every weekend with them and her sisters—who were even worse. I figure I would rather spend time with people I like—and just because I'm related to somebody doesn't mean I like them. [*Pause.*] I don't want to hurt Dan, but I have no idea how to, I don't know . . . I don't even know what we're supposed to do.

VENUS IN FUR
David Ives

Dramatic
VANDA, 20s

VANDA, *an actress, is auditioning for* THOMAS, *who has written
and is directing a play based on a notorious, sadomasochistic
19th-century novel. Her audition has become far more than just
an audition by this point, as she and* THOMAS *basically become
the characters in the novel, and as we begin to wonder if, perhaps,*
VANDA *is something far more than just an actress.*

VANDA   How does your Significant Other feel about this
   play? She's probably worried you've got this whole kinky
   side and she doesn't want you to put this play on because
   people will think this might be you. Or her. But let me
   guess about Stacy. She's a little younger than you. Good
   family. Grew up in one of those nice old stone houses.
   Maybe Connecticut. . . . Southwestern Massachusetts, near
   the Connecticut border. Twenty minutes from Litchfield.
   Am I close? She's tall. Maybe a little bossy, in a nice way.
   Lots of hair, long legs, big brain. Probably went to Stanford.
   Am I close? Maybe even a PhD. Well? She's got a dog. Let's
   see. Maybe a Weimaraner. That you like okay but could
   secretly do without, named something like . . . something
   traditional, something Old Testament and manly. Like . . .
   Seth. Ezra. I bet she's the breadwinner, too. I mean, a room
   with a pipe in the middle of it? Not exactly the big bucks
   on Broadway. She probably came with money, but while
   she finishes up her thesis she's working some nice invest-
   ment job. Or day-trading and making a fortune. Am I right?
   I'm right. But hey, you're an artist. She loves that about
   you. And she just knows you're going to be a great big

success someday. Plus she appreciates you for your sensitivity. Maybe you're the first guy she met who's got any. She reads a lot. Same books you do. Likes the opera and the ballet and shit. Like you. At night you talk about what's going on in French philosophy and what's new in the *New York Review of Books*, then you have some nice quiet sex. And nice quiet sex is fine. Though there's this rumbling at the back of your head. This voice that wants something else. I don't know what that is, but . . . *Rumble, rumble, rumble.* Anyway, hey, you're happy. You *like* her. You really, really like her and you two are going to have a nice life talking about French philosophy and what's in the *New York Review of Books* and maybe have a couple of kids who can do that when they grow up. And then you'll die.

WELCOME TO MY HEAD
Sam Bobrick

Seriocomic
ERIN, early 30s

ERIN *reprimands her husband,* GEORGE, *a playwright, for over-reaching in his choice of professions.*

ERIN   George, you're a big boy. For whatever reason, the choice to write whatever the hell you're writing was obviously yours. Frankly, I have no sympathy for writers who find themselves in these kinds of jams, where they lose focus of what they started out to do and then go into a panic mode like you're doing now. Life is too short for someone as exquisitely uncomplicated as myself to put up with this chaotic and desperate behavior, and I don't know how much longer I can or will. It's selfish and it's unfair. I don't want to upset you any more than you are, but it's very possible playwriting isn't for you. Your talent may not be as lofty as your ambition and once again you're overreaching. Maybe it's time to think about other areas that are not as demanding as the theater, like television for instance. That could solve everything. The expectations in that field are far less and the paychecks are far more. It's something to really consider. Anyway, I'm off to the gym. With any luck, when I get back, you'll have pulled yourself together and given what I just said some serious thought. Good-bye for now, George. I wish I could be more encouraging than honest. It's sometimes very confusing which is the more valued quality. Sometimes I really worry about you, even if it seems I don't.

WILD
Crystal Skillman

Seriocomic
NIKKI, 25

NIKKI, *an ex-dancer, nervous about the night, and about to have yet another hookup, tries to gain courage to open her heart again as she waits for* PETER, *who picked her up earlier that night.*

NIKKI   BE A FUCKING ADULT! That's what I wanted to scream at them. Fucking kids in the bar. Under age. You know they were. Nineteen-year-old pissant shit-faced—Don't. Don't stick up for them because they looked—. Because they were hot. With their [*Mimics clothes.*] and [*Mimics faces.*]. Whatever insecure glittery shit is exploding all over your apple-bottomed, jeaned ass, THEN TAKE THEM THE FUCK OFF, YOU TRENDY MOTHERFUCKER. Because yes—this twenty-five-year-old knows how to act in this fucking "cruel, cruel world." And if you don't act like who you are—who you really are. This world will. Eat you. Alive. I should go home. I shouldn't be here. I will. Go home. I'll—. Thought that the minute you came over, started talking. The minute you . . .

[*Imitates a simple gesture/movement Peter did that impressed her.*]

I was like "Oh, really" but wanted to. You are taking forever. Really? Really? It takes that long to fucking piss. You can't talk when you do it? That's insane. I talk when I shit all the time. Sometimes I find myself talking in the stall to myself. Other people. Depends on how much I take. I hate ecstasy. Sucks that's all you had. So nineties, whatever that was. My mom still only watches like Wynona Ryder movies. My mom's boyfriend, Phil: "Nikki, you look just like her" but I think that's just because I shoplift. Phil. He's retarded. A fucking joke. He's fucking blind as a bat but still shoots off guns in their backyard. He said he used to jerk off to her. Wynona Ryder. Kept pictures of her like under his bed in a shoebox. Now he's like forty-seven! Last class I took—Deconstructing the Twentieth Century—University of Chicago—my parents made me take fucking classes while at Joffrey—because how could I really make it—dancing—right!? "No one dances forever. Your body gives out—like that!—so you better be ready to figure out something else after."

WORSE THINGS
Mona Mansour

Dramatic
LIZ, early 30s

LIZ *is speaking to her girlfriend/partner,* MAEVE. *They've been to-gether for a few years, and while* MAEVE *likes to talk endlessly about their relationship, analyzing each and every minutiae of feeling,* LIZ *quite frankly finds this a buzzkill. They have started to fool around but got stopped because* MAEVE *wanted to "process," and* LIZ *has told* MAEVE *she'd rather talk about anything else than their relationship.*

LIZ   I just don't want to spend all our time talking about our sexual enjoyment. Every day, every WEEK, we spend time talking about our shit, our SEXUAL shit, whether we can fully relax or not. Why, why not, what it means to complete-ly GIVE IN, why we feel we can't, we have need to have time BEFORE, but not AFTER—before we need the tonal change, the tonal shift, into sex. And it's hard, because this world is fucked up and you get pushed in this world, just to go out and buy soy milk or whatever can be a trial, and you have to wear sunglasses to protect, to see out but not let them see *in* . . . my God—and in fact this same protective cover-ing is what we need to let go of when it's time to FUCK, be fucked, etcetera, and I gotta be careful not to use that word at the wrong time with you because some days it just hits you as dirty, the whole thing, and fuck or be fucked sounds either (a) crass or (b) like I'm just this suburban person trying to BE sexual and therefore (b1) that's even worse, because what's worse than an actual asexual, nonsexual, nonsexed person saying words like fuck, and so on? Noth-ing. I'm made needy, I'm made dirty, by saying that word. God I'm sick of myself.

YEAR OF THE ROOSTER
Eric Dufault

Comic
PHILIPA, 19

PHILIPA *is talking to her McDonald's coworker, a hapless middle-aged man named* GIL. *She tells him how and why she is going to get a managerial job instead of him. Then she tells him how she's going to celebrate.*

PHILIPA   See, the thing is, I'm a go-getter! I go, and I get! You don't need to be a dude, you don't need to be a slut, you don't need to graduate high school, all you need to know is what you want and go get it! I don't do coke, I don't do smack, and, now man, everything's coming up Philipa. Ten years from now, I'm gonna be like the manager of all McDonalds, and you know where I'm goin' after that? [*Beat.*] Walt Disney World Resort. You ever been to Walt Disney World Resort? Course ya haven't. I have literally met no one who went to Walt Disney World Resort. I bought this Disney autograph book when I was five? And when I go to Walt Disney World Resort, I'm gonna meet the dude who plays that little naked kid in *The Jungle Book*? Mowgli? And I'm gonna fuck the shit out of him. And after we've finished, I'll get him to sign my autograph book. And then, whenever any basic bitch tries to shame me or make me feel lesser than her or whatever, I'll show them the autograph book and be like: What've you done, bitch? And that's when I'll know I've made it.

PLAY SOURCES AND ACKNOWLEDGMENTS

To procure the entire text of a play, contact the rights holder.

ABOUT SPONTANEOUS COMBUSTION © 2012 by Sherry Kramer. Reprinted by permission of the author. For performance rights, contact Sherry Kramer (skramer@bennington.edu).

ADULT © 2011 by Christine Masciotti. Reprinted by permission of Antje Oegel, AO International. For performance rights, contact Antje Oegel (oaogel@aoegelinternational.com).

AEROSOL DREAMS © 2013 by Nicole Pandolfo. Reprinted by permission of the author. For performance rights, contact Lawrence Harbison (LHarbison1@nyc.rr.com).

AMERICA'S BRIGHTEST STAR © 2012 by Alex Goldberg. Reprinted by permission of the author. For performance rights, contact Alex Goldberg (alexstephengoldberg@gmail.com).

ANATOMIES © 2012 by Don Nigro. Reprinted by permission of the author. For performance rights, contact Samuel French, Inc. (212-206-8990; www.samuelfrench.com).

ANY DAY NOW © 2009 by Nat Cassidy. Reprinted by permission of the author. For performance rights, contact Nat Cassidy (natcassidy@gmail.com).

THE ASK © 2010 by David Lee White. Reprinted by permission of the author. For performance rights, contact David Lee White (david@passagetheatre.org).

BARRIO HOLLYWOOD © 2008 by Elaine Romero. Reprinted by permission of Bruce Ostler, Bret Adams Ltd. For performance rights, contact Bruce Ostler (bostler@bretadamsltd.net).

THE BEAUTIFUL DARK ©2013 by Erik Gernand. Reprinted by permission of Alexis Williams, Bret Adams Ltd. For performance rights, contact Alexis Williams (awilliams@bretadamsltd.net).

BETHANY © 2012 by Laura Marks. Reprinted by permission of Jessica Amato, The Gersh Agency. For performance rights, contact Dramatists Play Service, 440 Park Ave. S., New York, NY 10016 (212-683-8960; www.dramatists.com).

BIKE AMERICA © 2013 by Mike Lew. Reprinted by permission of Beth Blickers, Abrams Artists Agency. For performance rights, contact Beth Blickers (beth.blickers@abramsartny.com).

BITE ME © 2011 by Nina Mansfield. Reprinted by permission of the author. For performance rights, contact Nina Mansfield (nina@ninamansfield.com). The entire text is published by Smith and Kraus, Inc., in *2014: The Best 10-Minute Plays*.

BLACKTOP SKY © 2012 by Christina Anderson. Reprinted by permission of Bruce Ostler, Bret Adams Ltd. For performance rights, contact Bruce Ostler (bostler@bretadamsltd.net).

BOB: A LIFE IN FIVE ACTS © 2012 by Peter Sinn Nachtrieb. Reprinted by permission of Mark Orsini, Bret Adams Ltd. For performance rights, contact Dramatists Play Service, 440 Park Ave. S., New York, NY 10016 (212-683-8960; www.dramatists.com).

BRIDGE AND TUNNEL © 2012 by Anne Flanagan. Reprinted by permission of the author. For performance rights, contact Anne Flanagan (angrytimmypresents@yahoo.com).

BROADWAY OR BUST © 2013 by Rosary O'Neill. Reprinted by permission of Tonda Marton, The Marton Agency. For performance rights, contact Tonda Marton (tonda@martonagency.com).

BROKEN FENCES © 2011 by Steven Simoncic. Reprinted by permission of the author. For performance rights, contact Steven Simoncic (thirstyboots10@hotmail.com).

A COMMON MARTYR © 2013 by Michael Weems. Reprinted by permission of the author. For performance rights, contact Michael Weems (michaeltw721@gmail.com).

COMPLETENESS © 2011 by Itamar Moses. Reprinted by permission of Mark Subias, United Talent Agency. For performance rights, contact Samuel French, Inc. (212-206-8990; www.samuelfrench.com).

CONEY © 2012 by David Johnston. Reprinted by permission of the author. For performance rights, contact David Johnston (johnstondavidh@gmail.com).

CORE VALUES © 2013 by Steven Levenson. All rights reserved. CAUTION: professionals and amateurs are hereby warned that "Core Values" is subject to a royalty. It is fully protected under the copyright laws of the United States of America and of all countries covered by the International Copyright Union (including the Dominion of Canada and the rest of the British Commonwealth), the Berne Convention, the Pan-American Copyright Convention and the Universal Copyright Convention as well as all countries which the United States has reciprocal copyright relations. All rights, including professional/amateur stage rights, motion picture, recitation, lecturing, public reading, radio broadcasting, television, video or sound recording, all other forms of mechanical or electronic reproduction, such as CD-ROM, CD-1, information storage and retrieval systems and photocopying, and the rights of translation into foreign languages, are strictly reserved. Particular emphasis is laid upon the matter of readings, permission for which must be secured from the Author's agent in writing. Inquiries concerning performance rights should be addressed to: William Morris Endeavor Entertainment, LLC, 1325 Avenue of the Americas, New York, NY, 10019. Attn: John Buzzetti.

THE CURIOUS CASE OF THE WATSON INTELLIGENCE © 2013 by Madeleine George. Reprinted by permission of Seth Glewen, The Gersh Agency. For performance rights, contact Seth Glewen (sglewen@gershny.com).

CUT © 2012 by Crystal Skillman. Reprinted by permission of Amy Wagner, Abrams Artists Agency. For performance rights, contact Amy Wagner (amy.wagner@abramsartny.com).

DEACTIVATED © 2013 by Kimberly Pau. Reprinted by permission of the author. For performance rights, contact Kimberly Pau (kimberlypau@gmail.com).

DIFFERENT ANIMALS © 2012 by Abby Rosebrock. Reprinted by permission of the author. For performance rights, contact Abby Rosebrock (m.abigail.rosebrock@gmail.com).

THE DRUNKEN CITY © 2008 by Adam Bock. Reprinted by permission of ICM Partners. For performance rights, contact Samuel French, Inc. (212-206-8990; www.samuelfrench.com).

ELECTRA © 2011 by Don Nigro. Reprinted by permission of the author. For performance rights, contact Samuel French, Inc. (212-206-8990; www.samuelfrench.com).

EXQUISITE POTENTIAL © 2013 by Stephen Kaplan. Reprinted by permission of the author. For performance rights, contact Stephen Kaplan (stephen@bystephenkaplan.com).

THE FALLEN © 2010 by Yasmine Beverly Rana. Reprinted by permission of Susan Gurman, Susan Gurman Agency LLC. For performance rights, contact Susan Gurman (susan@gurmanagency.com).

THE FARM © 2010 by Walt McGough. Reprinted by permission of the author. For performance rights, contact Walt McGough (waltmcgough@gmail.com). The entire text is contained in *2014 New Playwrights: The Best Plays*, published by Smith and Kraus, Inc.

FIX ME, JESUS © 1994 by Helen Sneed. Reprinted by permission of the author. For performance rights, contact Dramatists Play Service, 440 Park Ave. S., New York, NY 10016 (212-683-8960; www.dramatists.com).

A GIRL'S GUIDE TO COFFEE © 2012 by Eric Coble. Reprinted by permission of Kate Navin, The Gersh Agency. For performance rights, contact Kate Navin (knavin@gershny.com).

H2O © 2012 by Jane Martin. Reprinted by permission of Mark Orsini, Bret Adams Ltd. For performance rights, contact Mark Orsini (morsini@bretadamsltd.net).

HARBOR © 2010 by Chad Beguelin. Reprinted by permission of Olivier Sultan, Creative Artists Agency. For performance rights, contact Olivier Sultan (osultan@caa.com).

HEADSTRONG © 2012 by Patrick Link. Reprinted by permission of the author. For performance rights, contact Patrick Link (patricklink1@gmail.com).

HOLOGRAM © 2011 by Don Nigro. Reprinted by permission of the author. For performance rights, contact Samuel French, Inc. (212-206-8990; www.samuelfrench.com).

HOME OF THE GREAT PECAN © 1997 by Stephen Bittrich. Reprinted by permission of the author. For performance rights, contact Stephen Bittrich (sbittrich@aol.com).

HONKY © 2014 by Greg Kalleres. Reprinted by permission of the author. For performance rights, contact Dramatists Play Service, 440 Park Ave. S., New York, NY 10016 (212-683-8960; www.dramatists.com). The play is also published by Smith and Kraus, Inc. in *2013 New Playwrights: The Best Plays*.

HOW WATER BEHAVES © 2012 by Sherry Kramer. Reprinted by permission of author. For performance rights, contact Sherry Kramer (skramer@bennington.edu).

JESUS IN INDIA © 2012 by Lloyd Suh. Reprinted by permission of Leah Hamos, Abrams Artists Agency. For performance rights, contact Leah Hamos (leah.hamos@abramsartny.com).

JIHAD JONES AND THE KALASHNIKOV BABES © 2008 by Yussef El Guindi. Reprinted by permission of Leah Hamos, Abrams Artists Agency. For performance rights, contact Leah Hamos (leah.hamos@abramsartny.com).